Peter Skillen

The Twelve-Step Warrior

Peter Skillen

About the Author

Peter Skillen was born in Leicester in the summer of 1970 and raised in the market town of Loughborough.

This is the story of his life.

Peter Skillen

Acknowledgments

I would like to thank the members of Alcoholics Anonymous around the world for always being there for me and for each other.

Thanks to Gloucester House and all the staff past and present for my recovery.

I would like to thank David Reed, my ever-present sponsor, for always having an open ear.

And my brothers and sisters for their wise words and unconditional love and support.

Thanks to Auntie Mary for all her hard work, help and advice.

And my lifelong best friends, Eamon Keating and Jason Hull. I value your friendship as much as life itself and I love you both.

I would like to thank Geoff Thompson and Collin S for making me believe in myself and inspiring me.

Thanks also to all my friends for encouraging me through five years of college and University. I love you all.

I would like to thank Jon Holmes and Tony Nichols, two of the most inspiring tutors you could ever wish to meet. They have helped me change my life and have brought new meaning to learning.

And finally, thanks to the John Skillen Martial Arts Gym and Fitness Centre Loughborough.

Peter Skillen

Peter Skillen

I dedicate this book to my mother, who was always my shining light in the darkness.

To my father, who was once lost but found his way back to leave an everlasting imprint on my life with his love and wise words.

And to my children: Jade, Amber, Daisy, Ava, Dexter and Ted.

Life is hard and the path is sometimes lonely, but press on, achieve your dreams and never give up!

I love you all.

"The war is constant and the battles are daily,

but I can never give up."

(Peter Skillen, 2011)

Peter Skillen

Contents

Foreword

I am honoured to write the foreword to this amazing book written by my friend Peter Skillen. I have known Peter for a number of years and have witnessed his painful climb from addiction, depression and destitution. It is hard to believe, and inspirational to see, how this once damaged man has become a successful filmmaker, a published author and a gentle and inspirational teacher.

I love him. Not just because he has had the courage to become a master of return, but also because he has had the courage to sit down and write this very personal story; a story that will bring light to countless others who find themselves in dark places. Escaping our past can be difficult enough, writing about our past in order to help others do the same is inspirational.

I highly recommend Peter Skillen. I highly recommend this book.

Read it, it may prove life-saving.

Geoff Thompson

BAFTA Award-winning writer, world-renowned martial artist and inspirational teacher.

Peter Skillen

Preface

Did you ever go to the cinema with a friend to see a film you absolutely loved, only to find out when the movie ended that your friend hated it?

Two people can share the same experience and, while one might be having the time of their life, the other might be living a nightmare.

Your memories will be different from mine. Although you may share the same experience with another person or many other people, your memories of that experience will be different.

Memories are snapshots of time stored in the brain that allow us, with a little effort, to relive past experiences. They can be played out like short films over and over again in the cinema of the mind.

This is a book full of such memories, my memories, and while it was hard to write them down it is something I had to do.

I pass these memories on to you in the hope that they may in some way help you or someone you know to become free from bondage, whatever that bondage may be.

Peter Skillen

Peter Skillen

Prologue

For most of my young life I searched for a meaning to my existence. I lived on the very edge of society and, like my fellow outcasts, made the mistake of looking for answers in the wrong places.

I know now that I didn't stand a chance of finding a worthwhile existence living among the thieves, fighters, gamblers and onetime somebodies who propped up the bars of the worst drinking holes. But back then, I didn't recognise that these people had already given up on life or that I had fallen into their fold.

I lived from one alcohol hit to the next. My craving for it consumed me. Working out how to get a drink took over my daily existence, to the point that even when I had achieved my goal and stood looking at a full glass, I had no peace. I was obsessed with plotting and planning where I could get my next one from.

The compulsive nature of my disease brought me to my knees. I lost everything. Instead of being in the company of my family and true friends, I chose to rub shoulders with the walking dead.

Loneliness engulfed me when I made my way to my empty excuse for a home each night. But once there I would welcome the ability to fall into the black pit of unconsciousness.

This book will tell you how all of this came to pass and how, after drawing on my very last reserves, I turned my life around.

One

Early Home Life

Looking back on my childhood years, I hold many good memories dear. But at the same time those reminiscences are powerful and often painful reminders of the beginning of my journey to hell and back.

I did not enter a lonely world. Born in Leicestershire in 1970 to a beautiful mother and hardworking father, I had four brothers and two sisters waiting for me.

My first memories are of the walls of our home vibrating with fun, laughter and happiness. Mum, with her shoulder-length, shiny brown hair framing her lovely face and enhancing her creamy, glowing complexion, always had a smile to light up our day. The daily grind of taking care of us all never fazed her. I adored her and spent most of my time attached to her hip.

My dad, a thick-set Irishman, was not very tall, but had a strong stature, jet black hair, liquid blue eyes and a good measure of the blarney that charmed everyone he met. He took great pride in his appearance, although his hairstyle never kept up with current trends as he styled it after the 1950s teddy boys, with a small quiff at the front and a 'DA' (duck's arse) at the back. Back then, a bet on the horses or dogs, a couple of pints on a Friday night and the love he had for his wife and family made him a happy man.

This was a good world full of love for a little boy to grow up in, but one that I would see degenerate, leaving me to fight against the odds for my self-worth and sense of direction.

The Friday night ritual of Dad and Mum going out to the local pub, leaving me and my closest siblings in age, Sam and James, in the care of our sister Helen, gave me my first taste of fear. I can't remember my eldest brothers, Joseph and John, or my sister Bernadette, who was just younger than them, being around much at this time, but as they were already in their teens I assume they were out and about doing their own thing.

The first trickle of trepidation entered me as Dad stood waiting in the hallway for Mum while she kissed us all one by one. She was reluctant to leave us and Dad would have to hurry her along. I didn't want them to go. The house took on a different feel without them present, but Helen soon dispelled my panic.

She dispatched Sam to fetch blankets from upstairs and James to get coal and kindling from the coal shed. Then she would resort to all kinds of tricks to get the fire going: from blowing at the small sparks, to wafting them, to standing the coal shovel in the hearth and covering it with a sheet of newspaper to create a vacuum. Sometimes when she did this the paper caught fire and Helen would push it into the fireplace. The draught sucked it up the chimney, leaving a trail of glowing hot soot on the back of the fire, and the room filled with smoke.

Snuggled under blankets munching on crushed biscuits that we washed down with the warm milk Helen had prepared for us helped some of the tension to seep out of me. However, it swiftly returned as the late night horror film lulled them all to sleep, while I was left wide awake and feeling alone.

Then the room took on a sinister life of its own. Dancing shadows from the flickering black and white television, together with the bright orange glow of the burning embers, licked the centre of the walls, leaving the corners dark and eerie. My imagination turned my home into a terrifying, lonely place and I would pull my feet up under the blanket to make sure none of my skin was exposed.

Soon the programmes ended and the national anthem filled the space around me. The white noise of the television hissed and crackled, adding to the dread inside me. My heart beat faster and I prayed for the return of my mum and dad.

After what seemed like hours of sitting, scared out of my wits, the sounds of the key in the front door and the laughter of my mum were welcome ones.

As the door opened, the cold wind blew in an aroma like no other: a slight smell of perfume mixed with stale cigarette smoke and a hint of beer breath, plus the Holy Grail of Mum and Dad's return: chips wrapped in newspaper.

With Dad sitting in his chair, Helen perched on the arm next to him and us boys on the settee with Mum, the sound of ripping paper enhanced the anticipation inside me as Mum made small squares filled with a few chips for each of us.

I can still remember the delicious burst of flavour filling my mouth as I bit into the first chip. We all took as much time as we could to devour them as we sought to delay the inevitable bedtime that would follow.

All of this happened to a background of Mum boasting to Dad and the rest of us about how she had beaten all the men at pool. Chomping on my chips listening to her and just feeling her close turned the room that had petrified me into a place that now shrouded me in love and warmth.

Eventually, all tactics played out, it was time to go to bed. Helen and the two lads kissed Dad goodnight and two loving arms gathered me up, making everything right with my world once more as Mum took me over to Dad for my goodnight kiss. As I leant down I knew what would happen. I would be a giggling mess as Dad cupped my face and rubbed the bristles of his stubble-covered chin up and down my cheeks in a playfully rough but loving way. I always loved it when he did this, and it prompted the affectionate nickname of 'old bristle face'.

Shrieks of laughter would meet us as Mum carried me upstairs. Sam and James would be play-wrestling. They would fight to get the spot nearest the wall, knowing that the conquering hero would have no chance of losing his share of the covers or falling out of bed. The ritual resembled two lion cubs learning to fight in order to survive in the wilds of the jungle. Little did Sam and James realise that this was schooling for what would happen later in our lives, albeit in a different kind of jungle!

Although I joined in the tussle, in reality I always wanted to be in the middle where I felt safest. But then, with the calm of a settled argument, came the rude awakening of the freezing cold sheets as our legs went into action kicking up and down to warm them up. In the wintertime, with central heating unheard of in council houses, coats would be thrown over the top of the blankets for extra warmth. At those times, when the bitter cold seeped into the house, ice would form on the inside of the windows.

Now snuggled down with the covers right up under our chins, we listened to Mum as she led us in our evening prayers. We would say the Lord's Prayer, the Hail Mary and Glory Be to the Father, followed by the blessings, which went on so long it felt as though she was going to ask God to bless everybody in the whole wide world. One sentence at a time, she would say: "God bless Mum and Dad, Granny and Granddad, all my brothers and sisters, all my friends and relations, all sick people in hospital. Thank you for looking after me today. Sorry if I've been a naughty boy; I'll try and be a good boy tomorrow. Matthew, Mark, Luke and John, bless this bed that I lay on." We would repeat each sentence after her. Then, once she had finished, she would slowly back out the room, leaving the door ajar in case any of us should wake in the night.

Weekday mornings brought a hectic commotion loud enough to awaken a hibernating bear. All the family congregated in the kitchen, trying to glean some warmth from the only source of heating in the house at that hour: the lit gas rings and the open oven door. The air filled with the smell of toast as huge quantities passed from Mum to the table for a short-lived existence, followed by hot tea from what seemed like a bottomless teapot.

Getting ready for school was a free-for-all, but eventually everyone set off. The older ones would walk the three miles to **De Lisle** Roman Catholic Comprehensive School and Mum would walk me to St Mary's Catholic Primary School.

Sam and James didn't like going to school as Mum couldn't afford the uniform and the other kids teased them. Most of the kids at the schools we went to were better off than us Shelthorpe kids and had never had the pleasure of wearing hand-me-downs. They found it funny that we wore patched-up trousers and shoes with our toes poking out the ends. Many a day Sam and James came home with tales of how one of the teachers had punished them with the cane across the back of their legs for fighting with kids who had taken the piss.

I learned later that trying to explain the feelings of humiliation to teachers was impossible. They had no sympathy and many of them berated us themselves at the first opportunity.

But although we lacked food, heating and money for school clothes, we were happy. Every night, us kids played games like blind man's bluff together or climbed the two apple trees that stood in our back yard. On a Sunday evening, Mum stoked up the fire and ran us a hot bath, and then a mad half-hour followed as we ran around the house. Those nights were always full of laughter and I am grateful to have the memory of them, as they did not last.

Two

The Kids of Manor Drive

We lived in a five-bedroomed council property on Manor Drive; a horseshoe-shaped road on Shelthorpe Council Estate. It was a large estate that housed many colourful characters: a mixture of those who worked hard, those who drew state benefits and those who did both!

Our huge garden backed on to Charlie Baxter's. Charlie looked like an old man should in his flat cap, tweed trousers and waistcoat. Every morning I made my way to the fence that separated our gardens to watch him tend to and gather his crop of wonderful fruit and vegetables. I listened, enthralled, as he told me how each vegetable grew and what he would be planting next. Just before he went back into his house he always threw me a couple of apples or gave me some freshly picked rhubarb that I would wash and dip in sugar before I ate it. I loved Charlie and I miss him to this day.

At this time, and with me still being very young, Saturday brought one of the highlights of my week. The bed never pulled at me on Saturday as I had cartoons to watch on television: *Top Cat* and *Scooby-Doo*, and later *Tiswas* and *World of Sport Wrestling*. But in between these came a film that gave me more excitement than all of these shows put together: the Saturday morning matinee of *The Legend of Tarzan, Lord of the Apes*. And it wasn't just any old Tarzan. It had to be Johnny Weissmuller. As the credits rolled, the anticipation built inside me, reaching a crescendo at the orchestral rendering of the theme tune.

I became Tarzan, even to the point of wearing swimming

trunks under my trousers for the moment when I would need to strip off and launch into action. The sofa became a hill I had to jump over and cushions posed as deadly enemies, crocodiles and lions that I had to fight and conquer. Jane's high-pitched scream not only alerted Tarzan, it sent me into a frenzy as I too, the Lord of the Jungle, had to rescue her. Off came my top clothes and with my freckled face and golden curls I would stretch to my full two-and-a-half feet, beat my chest and call out: "Arrrghhh, Arrrgghhaaa, Arrrgghhaaa!" It didn't get better than this!

In the distance I would hear the sound of horns. Was this a stranded riverboat or a trapped explorer trying to get my attention? No, it was Russell's Grocery Bus doing its Saturday morning rounds. I needed no further prompt to abandon Jane. Sprinting as quickly as Tarzan, I would grab 10p from Mum and run out to the ageing 1960s coach Mr Russell had converted into a mobile shop. Inside, the shelves held everything from bread and milk to bleach and polish, but most importantly, sweets! Many a Manor Drive kid was brought up on Mr Russell's 10p mix.

As I walked up the silver, chequer-plate steps, Mr Russell's voice commanded: "Make way for Tarzan, everyone!" Then he would hand me my little white paper bag. Mr Russell was my mate and would often put a few extra sweets in for me. The thought of the treat that was in store brought me back down to earth. No swinging in the trees or rescues could go on until I had devoured the contents of my bag, which I did sitting on a grass verge while watching the ants scurrying around in the mid-morning sun.

Over the years, life in Manor Drive had its ups and downs, but they were mostly good times. And despite the reputation it had for being a rough place, the people who lived there were real people; people who didn't stand to one side and watch you struggle if you fell on hard times or were stuck in a rut, but were there for you and would help you before you even needed to ask.

It seemed as if a hundred kids lived on our street and we all played together. We would build trolleys for racing and go to the local orchards to scrump apples. The cornfields surrounding our estate became a playground heaven for us, but sometimes a bigger adventure beckoned and we would venture across the fields to the woods about five miles away.

First we would have to hold a 'meeting', with every kid on the street assembled. This included my brothers Sam and James; Andy and Benji Johnson, whose mother was one of the street's many matriarchs; the McConnells, Brian and Sweeney, two of the best piss-takers in the world; the Pepper brothers, Gary, who was the oldest and a great footballer, Johnny, who was the smallest of the elder lot, Andy, who was the youngest; and Dinesh, our next-door neighbour. He had recently arrived from Uganda and was a sound lad who took great pride in making my dad roar with laughter every time he told him that Idi Amin was "a fuck-pig".

The older lads began by organising the adventure in the woods. Then everyone pooled their small amounts of pocket money. This 'kitty' was entrusted to us younger kids and we went off to the local shop and bought biscuits and fizzy pop; vital refreshments for later. Like a convoy of explorers, we would leave our street through an allotment at the end of the road and head across the fields and streams towards Beacon Hill, a beautiful country park that stands majestically above my hometown of Loughborough.

Excitement and anticipation filled me every time we started out, as memories of earlier trips to Beacon Hill promised a great day's entertainment. The talk would revolve around who would be first to reach the summit or the one who would dare to climb the highest rocks. We snapped branches off trees to use as walking sticks or for sword fighting. The older lads – Sam, Andy, Brian, Gaz and Sweeney – walked at the front of the group and I liked to walk with them, feeling like one of the leaders.

At last we would arrive at the entrance to the woods; a barbed wire fence at the end of a cornfield. One of the older lads held up the bottom of the wire and we would file underneath it one by one. Once inside we ran around shouting and screaming, climbing the trees and the massive rock face at the top of the hill. Here we had freedom away from the confines of the red-brick council estate. Nothing mattered.

Team games shaped our character as we played in the bracken and the undergrowth. These were the days of long, hot summers and we were happy and free from worries. As night fell, a rag-tag band of hungry, thirsty and tired boy soldiers trekked homeward.

Three

A Terrifying Ordeal

One such outing didn't have a happy ending. Sam and James went off to do their own thing, leaving me to go home on my own. I returned to find no one in.

The house became a place of fear for me once more. Maybe this was because of the stories my elder brothers and sisters had told me about it being haunted, or maybe it was just because of the silence that day compared with when everyone was in. Whatever it was, I just couldn't be in there, so I went outside and sat on the grass verge, amusing myself by digging in the dirt with an old lollipop stick.

An older lad from the street came over to me and sat down. After a moment he asked me if I wanted to go up to the allotment for a bit to see a den he had built. I had no thoughts that I shouldn't, and it would pass the time, anyway.

His den resembled those all of us had built from time to time. At the end of summer harvest we would gather up the straw from a nearby field and cover the hedgerow with it to form special places of our own. I followed him into his. Cosy and smelling of freshly cut straw, it welcomed me and dispelled that earlier 'home alone' feeling. I admired his handiwork, unaware of what he had in mind.

It started as a play fight. Without warning, he jumped on me. There was nothing unusual in that, we all loved wrestling. Often we pretended we were Giant Haystacks or Big Daddy, a pair of famous wrestlers from the 1970s.

But then the wrestling turned from play into reality. I stung with the force of his punches and choked as his fingers tightened around my throat. He ignored my pleas for him to stop. Pain seared me. I wanted to escape, but I couldn't.

He sat on my chest, his weight crushing me, and I thought I was going to choke. I tried in desperation to push him off me, but he was too heavy. He held my arms down by my sides, his full body weight bearing down on my chest. I couldn't breathe and panic filled me. My tears turned to sobs.

He trapped my arms under his knees as I struggled with all my might, gasping for air. Horror gripped me as he sat back and I heard the sound of a zip being undone. Unable to look away, I watched as he took out his cock. With one hand holding my forehead and the other grabbing my throat, he forced my head backwards and shoved it into my mouth. I couldn't move. I couldn't hear anything or make any noise. I was suffocating.

Suddenly, he jumped up and ran off. I lay frozen to the spot; silence engulfed me. My mind replayed the incident as though it had happened in slow motion. I snapped out of my daze, jumped to my feet and ran.

Mum shouted out to me as I entered our house, but there was only one place I wanted to be; the one place where I could lock the world away. The moment the catch clicked I slumped onto the cold, red-tiled floor of the toilet.

A scared and confused seven-year-old, I sat screwed up in a ball and cried for half an hour. The tears flowed terrifying images flashed through my mind. Every bit of my body trembled with fear.

I felt weak and pathetic as I had no answers to the questions pounding around my head: 'Why did he do this to me? Why couldn't I stop him?'

Eventually, Mum knocked on the door. I didn't want her to see me, so I told her the lock was stuck. The handle shook as she tried to open it. Then I knew I actually wanted to be with her. I wiped my eyes and slid the lock across.

"There you go," she said, as I ran out of the door and into her arms. "What's wrong?"

I fobbed her off by telling her I was scared when I realised I couldn't open the door.

"You silly bugger," she said. "You should have shouted me."

I hugged her for what seemed like an eternity, until she released herself from me and went into the loo.

I climbed the stairs to my room. As young as I was, I knew I had crossed a line in my life. No longer the innocent, joyful child, my whole world had changed and I felt as though that grotesque incident had ripped away my happiness and left me empty. I cried myself to sleep.

Shame prevented me from telling anyone about the incident, but my sense of fun disappeared as if someone had switched a light off inside of me. I no longer wanted to go out into the street with the others. I felt different from them, like an outcast, and no matter where I was or what I was doing, that feeling of separation followed me. I could not resolve the constant battle inside me; I could not shake the feeling that I should not have let it happen.

Nightmares crept into my sleeping hours. Sweating with the terror they brought me, my sobs woke the whole house. Mum's attempts to comfort me only made me feel worse. Pangs of guilt mixed with my humiliation until, exhausted, I fell asleep in her arms to wake up the next morning snuggled up to her in her bed.

At that time mum had two jobs. In the mornings she cleaned for a lovely lady named Mrs Ashmore. Sometimes Mum took me with her and at other times Helen took care of me. This had never bothered me before; I had quite happily stayed with my sister and brothers.

But now I never wanted to be out of my mum's sight. My sense of dread manifested itself in screams. I would shout and try to fight my way out of the house, or I would run to the only place I felt secure, the toilet, which had become my sanctuary. Once locked in this small space with nowhere for anyone to conceal themselves or have any way of getting to me, I could try to hide from the feeling of fear that had taken up permanent residence inside me.

But one day even being in there failed me. I could not calm myself. Trepidation shook my body and panic engulfed me. The feeling was so great it crushed my spirit and I had to get out. Not just out of the toilet, but out of the house. However, if I opened the toilet door I knew Helen and my brothers would stop me from leaving.

The small, frosted window above my head offered me my only route of escape. Getting through it posed a challenge as, when open, the gap was no bigger than two feet wide and one foot high. Climbing onto the toilet bowl I dragged myself up onto the window ledge. My small frame stood me in good stead on this occasion, as I managed to put one leg through the window, then my head, before finally pulling my other leg through. Free at last, I fled to Mrs Ashmore's house; a beautiful old Tudor property, which, though not far from us, stood in a different world.

Shock registered on my mother's face when she answered the door. I flung myself at her, telling her I didn't want to stay home without her. Mrs Ashmore invited me in and made me tea and toast while Mum finished vacuuming the carpets. When we arrived home, my brothers and sister couldn't believe I was with Mum. They had thought I had fallen asleep in the toilet!

That lost feeling whenever my Mum left the house prompted me to invent many ways of escaping our house if she went out. One time she caught the bus to go shopping and I ran after her so fast that when she arrived in town she found me waiting for her at the bus stop! Being with her made me feel protected.

Four

Life Begins to Crumble

The beginning of the end arrived with the fitting of a bar in our front room. Soon after this, all of the furniture either found its way into the yard or was squashed against the walls to make room for a full-sized table tennis table. Our house turned into a pub; open all hours and rocking to the beat of the Rod Stewart songs that blasted out of the stereo.

My dad's friend Alan started visiting every night, bringing wine and beer with him, and chaos reigned. Fuelled by the ever-present beer, Dad lived in a state of drunkenness. He seemed compelled to shout about his past achievements as if they made up for the present. I listened as he boasted about how he had once been the best boxer in Ireland, while Mum whooped and danced around the room.

My brothers played table tennis until the early hours of the morning, and me? Well, the freedom to do as I liked went down well at first, especially as the carefree adults thought it was OK to give me the odd glass of sherry.

The sweet, sticky wine became like nectar to me. I loved it and would refill my glass when Dad wasn't looking. It had a comforting effect as I sat and wondered what had happened to my loving mum and dad as they became just shadows of their former selves.

Warmed by the sherry and giggling at things I wouldn't normally find funny, I went along with it all until, as always, the night came to an end with everyone shouting and swearing. Then I would run up to my bed, pull the covers over me and beg God to stop this madness and make things return to normal.

They didn't. They just changed. An argument between my sister and Alan, which ended when the police arrived, brought an end to the front room pub. The table tennis table went and the parties were no more. But with the demise of our own bar, the excessive drinking took a new turn. Instead of whooping it up at home, Mum and Dad went to the local pub every night. Mum was getting just as drunk as Dad, only she was better at hiding it.

And so, after a summer spent in the front room bar and coping with the deterioration in my parents and family life, the school term began once more.

Sam and James hadn't been attending school and our family now had a social worker. The headmistress at my school, Sister Mary David – a nun of some repute, who had a reputation for ruling the school with an iron fist (and a bamboo cane) – came into my class one day when I was about eight years old and asked for me by name. My legs shook as I followed her and I tried to think what I had done wrong.

She took me to the staff room and she and another teacher sat me down. They informed me that the authorities had taken Sam and James into a care home because of their truancy. I burst into tears, imagining my brothers locked away in a large prison cell and that I would never see them again. I remember expecting my mum to turn up and console me, to explain what had happened, but she never came. Instead, I walked home alone, crying and wondering what would become of me, as it seemed as though my whole family had fallen apart. One by one they were deserting me.

A few weeks later, Mum took me to Leicester to visit Sam and James. James was in a grand house set in wooded grounds, aptly named 'The Woodlands'. It had the feel of a private school, and that day it had a festive feel as they were holding a garden fete.

Ironically, James had the job of running a small raffle stall. Unbeknown to the staff there he had sold raffle tickets on behalf of his real school to raise money for a new roof a year or so before. Only, on that occasion, the prize draw didn't take place as James kept all the money for himself. This enterprise had earned him the nickname 'Raffles' after the gentleman-thief from a popular television series of the same name.

Mum won a sack of spuds from James's stall, and later that week James delivered them himself with one of the carers from the kids' home.

On the face of things, The Woodlands appeared a happy place, but underneath it held a dark secret that came to light years later when some of its ex-residents had the courage to blow the whistle. This resulted in those involved paying for their sins through the justice system.

***

We found out they had taken Sam to a very different place in another part of the city. Here we entered a rough, dark and dirty house, where the kids all ran wild. Mum couldn't believe the filthy state of it. She asked if Sam could come with us into Leicester and the women in charge agreed. As soon as we were out of the area, Mum hatched her plan. She told Sam he wasn't going back there and then she took us to The Woodlands to fetch James.

When we arrived they told us he had been in trouble and that they had locked him in the secure room. Mum had no choice but to take us home and to leave James, as we now know, in the hands of disgusting people who, instead of looking after the children, treated them like animals.

Sam had to go back to the children's home, but they released him a few months later. James, who had tried to escape many times, wasn't so lucky. He now resided in a secure unit. This didn't stop him, though, and he often escaped and came back home as Sam had. As a result, we constantly had social workers and police at our house looking for them.

I once dug a big trench about four feet deep in our back garden so that I could play soldiers and I covered it over with wood to conceal it. One night when Sam and James were on the run from the police they hid in the trench and pulled the wood over themselves.

One of the policemen actually stood on top of the wooden cover and I'll never know how he didn't fall through it into my trench. He shouted out to my brothers, telling them he would find them, not knowing that they were right under his feet.

It was a cold winter that year, and at home we had nothing to combat the bitter cold. The gas and electricity board had switched off our power due to unpaid bills. The house felt like the inside of a freezer. Ice formed on the insides of the windows and we could see our breath as it made fine vapour clouds when we spoke.

Unable to bear it one night, my mum and brothers took the doors off a couple of the rooms and broke them up to make fuel for the fire. It might seem to others that this defeated the object, but it didn't as the doors had had that many holes punched in them during arguments that we didn't notice any extra draught without them in place.

The winter brought an early end to the daylight hours, and the fear of the dark I had had since babyhood still hadn't left me. Rather, it had intensified after the theft of my innocence. So when, as often happened, I returned home from school to an empty, cold and soulless house, panic shortened my breath and a feeling of suffocation gripped me. Staying home alone wasn't an option, and as always I had to find Mum and be somewhere near her.

Leaving our garden and running out of our street as fast as I could, I would grind to a halt when I came to the recreation park, or 'recky' as we called it. Here my courage faced a further test, because at night the recky was a scary place.

A long, black footpath ran through its centre. Heart thumping, I would stand for a moment at the start of it until, knowing that I had to do it, I summoned up all the courage I could muster and ran like the wind along what the local lads called 'The Devil's Footpath'. My tears of fear stung as the cold air dried them in silver streaks across my cheeks.

Once I reached the shops on the other side, across the road from the pub, I stood for a moment and bathed in the reassuring lights that shone from the street lamps while I caught my breath and wiped my face.

Opening the door to the bar released a warm draft of alcohol and smoke-filled air. It was a smell I knew well and it was one that soothed me with its familiarity. All I had to do now was catch Mum's eye. When I did and she came outside to me, I would beg her to come home. She would always tell me that she wouldn't be long before going back inside and returning with beef-flavoured crisps and a bottle of pop.

Dad never came out. It wasn't because he didn't want to; he was just so drunk he didn't even know I was there. When Mum left me to go back inside I would lean against the wall and wait in the place I hated most in the world: outside the fucking Bull's Head.

As young as I was, I could hate with a passion. The Bull's Head represented everything that had ruined my childhood. It lured away those who should have taken care of us. Its yellowing walls enclosed adults who had abandoned all hope and their own kids, too, for that matter; adults who spent their days propping up the bar, talking about how hard times were and how money was so scarce.

It seemed funny to me that dinner tables all across the estate were empty, while pint glasses were always full. In our house, the piles of toast we used to enjoy for breakfast had dwindled and now we were limited to a single slice. Sometimes there would be no bread in the house and we would have to run to the neighbours and ask them for a few slices. Our evening meal was usually a stew and homemade soda bread. It was delicious, but the small quantities meant that we often went to bed hungry.

Some nights, other kids that had been left to fend for themselves would join me outside the pub. We must have looked a right motley crew, shivering from the cold and trying to appease our grumbling tummies with bags of crisps, while our parents paid for the landlord's Jaguar, his wife's twice-yearly holidays and a growing collection of gold chains and designer dresses.

Now and then a treat would come our way as some blokes would slip us 10p for sweets on their way into the pub. And it wasn't all without fun. Being almost 'street urchins' equipped us with a resourcefulness that often led to nice little earners.

Just before Bonfire Night one year, a couple of the lads who were hanging around outside the pub had a Halloween mask. After having a bit of a joke with it, we stopped and watched a group of kids across the street in front of the shops. They had made a Guy Fawkes dummy, which slumped on the pavement in front of them while they, like little Oliver Twists, held out a cap. Their calls of "Penny for the Guy" were coining it in for them.

We decided we wanted some of the action, but we had no Guy. And then it dawned on us. A couple of hours later we had amassed about a tenner in change and had the best Guy in the area. Everyone commented on how realistic it looked and how well made it was. What they didn't realise was that the other two lads had stuffed my sleeves with newspaper, stuck the Halloween mask over my face and pulled my hood up. We laughed all the way to the chip shop and ate our fill.

To finance such treats on other nights we would drag carrier bags of cider bottles from our homes. These empties, which had topped up our already-drunk parents after their night out, had a refund value of 5p each if they were returned to the pub. On the odd occasion we didn't have any, we scaled the wall of the pub yard, stole a couple of crates and cashed them back in.

At Christmas time our sweet, boyish voices rang out as we sang carols around the richer neighbourhoods. Singing "We Three

Kings" or "Away in a Manger" while our breath came out like steam on a frosty night had them all feeling sorry for us and they would give us money or a few sweets.

One night we were singing outside a really large house and an old lady answered the door. She said she loved the sound of our voices and asked us to go inside and sing by the Christmas tree. I wouldn't, but a few of the other lads did. I looked in through the window and nearly wet myself laughing as I watched them writhing with embarrassment. They had to sing in front of the tree to about ten members of her family.

Some of my laughter was a cover for the tinge of envy I felt. I was looking into a world I had never experienced. It wasn't that Christmas hadn't ever been great in our house, because up until then, it had. There had always been loads of toys for us kids and plenty of food.

The only problem was, Mum would be repaying it all year at the rate of a couple of quid each week from one of the legal loan sharks that preyed on the struggling families on our estate.

These leeches sold food hampers and charged extortionate rates of interest, and they knew they could get away with it because everyone in the area was so broke their only other choice was to go without. What followed was a weekly visit from the shark, with us kids having to make excuses up for our parents on the weeks when they were penniless. While they hid behind the sofa or upstairs we would be telling the shark, "Me mum ain't in."

On one occasion me, Mum, Sam and James hid behind the sofa in the front room while the shark knocked at the front door. Mum shushed us all, trying not to make a sound as she had run out of excuses. We kids just giggled. Mum relaxed when the knocking stopped and it had gone quiet, joining in with our giggling.

All of a sudden there was a voice at the window. The shark hadn't gone away; he had walked round the house and was peering in at us as we sat huddled behind the sofa. With a sarcastic smile on his face and his nose pressed against the glass, he casually said, "I'll pop back tomorrow." Mum was mortified, but we found it hilarious that the shark had caught her out.

One Christmas Eve when times were really hard, my sister Bernadette and I went to the local golf course and cut down a Christmas tree. We dragged it back over the fields only to find when we got it home that we couldn't get it through the front door. We cut it down, dragged it inside, made some paper decorations and topped it with the lights and a fairy we had had for years. It looked brilliant and the spare wood from the trunk came in handy as fuel for the fire. But despite this festive touch, our cupboards were empty and our Christmas looked bleak.

That all changed on the return of Sam and James, who had been out all night. They came in with bags full of frozen food and sweets. They told Mum they had found a bag of money and been out shopping. They had saved our Christmas! We all ate well and had presents.

A few days later, in between Christmas and New Year, the local copper knocked at the door and asked for Sam and James. He said there had been a burglary at the local Co-op store on Christmas Eve and that they had reason to believe Sam and James had been involved.

Mum was horrified. The copper looked at us all as we stood just inside the door. Without explanation, he told my mum they had probably got it wrong and then he left. Maybe he felt sorry for us, or maybe the Christmas spirit got to him, I will never know.

That winter was one of the hardest I can remember, but somehow we siblings got through it with the help of Mum, who, though on the wrong path, still found time for us. In her own way she was there for us during the roughest of it. One cuddle from her could still make everything right in my world.

Five

The Downward Spiral

I soon faced even more changes as the time came to move up from St Mary's Catholic Infant School on Gray Street to St Mary's Catholic Junior School on Hastings Street, which was on the other side of town. I had to make the daily trek on my own across the allotments and fields; a trip made even more daunting on wet days as my feet squelched in the mud, blackening and damping my socks as it soaked through the flap where the sole had come away from the top of my shoe.

My first day set the pattern of what I look back on as the piss-taking years. I entered a playground full of fellow 'newbies', all of whom were milling around in their pristine new uniforms, and I immediately became the target of their smirks and whispers behind hands as my small body shrank even further into my two-sizes-too-big, hand-me-down blazer.

Most of the insults came from my peers, but the teachers also had a way with words. Mr Taylor, a tall, ginger-haired man who wore small round glasses and could have been a model for the teachers in Pink Floyd's "Another Brick in the Wall" video, did his fair share of ridiculing, but he came nowhere near the cruel Mr Uscavage.

Uski, as we called him, was one of life's true bastards. He was a mean man who held in him something alien to his chosen profession: an innate dislike of children. Every kid in the school feared and hated him in equal measure. He took no prisoners, but he picked on me more than the rest, latching on to my vulnerability and amusing my fellow pupils at my expense.

His total loathing of me came to the boil one day when I answered a question incorrectly and he mocked me in front of the whole class. Unable to take it, I challenged him. His face changed and his stride towards me told of my doom. His bony hands grabbed my jacket and resistance was useless. He dragged me out into the cloakroom and, with his face close to mine, threatened to "punch my lights out". Those were his exact words. He then grabbed me tightly by my shirt collar and choked me to near unconsciousness before stopping as suddenly as he had started.

Left there sitting on a wooden bench among the damp-smelling coats, my body shook with my sobs and I wondered what I had done to cause him to have such a deep-seated hatred of me. But that incident didn't become an isolated one and I came to despise him more and more each time he demonstrated his loathing towards me. As a teacher, he was the worst of the worst.

The only respite I had from all of this came from Mr Coleman, the sports teacher. Although he had the same sarcastic way of speaking as the rest of them, he was a different type altogether. A giant of a man with curly black hair and a moustache, he wouldn't have looked out of place in an old '70s movie. He treated the kids in a totally different way. He was no pushover, but he had a way of telling you off that let you know he cared about the lads in his charge. He commanded a little respect and he got it. In my opinion, he deserved it, too.

Coping with verbal bullying wasn't the only cross I had to bear at Hastings Street. I also found the work rate much more intense than at Gray Street and I started to struggle. I was fine at doing simple maths and English, but bigger problems confused me. I'd ask for help and understood while they explained things to me, but when I came to do it by myself I found I hadn't got a clue.

This bewildered me, as I didn't know why I couldn't retain the information. Recently this question has been answered, as I now know I have dyslexia and am at the high end of the scale. A few of the teachers showed their frustration at my constant questions and often just said, "Get on with it, Skillen", or in Uski's case, "Are you thick, Skillen?" Then he would compound the insult by laughing at me. My hatred for him and my unhappiness led me to start skipping school.

Some days I just couldn't face it. On the occasions when Mum couldn't be persuaded that I didn't feel well, I would leave the house and head in the right direction, but instead of going to school I would walk along the riverbanks around the outskirts of Loughborough or hide away in the derelict buildings on one of the estates.

As I was on free school dinners I had no money or food, but I kept myself entertained during the long, hungry hours by making up stories and having imaginary adventures. I liked the loneliness of those days away from the misery of school and the shouting and craziness of my house.

Among all the insults and the feeling that I was inadequate and thick, I had one saving grace: my friend Phil. Phil didn't see me as different and didn't mind being associated with me. He even invited me to his birthday parties. He lived in a nice big house full of warmth and love and – on these occasions – lots of jelly, ice cream and orange squash!

After one such event, filled to bursting and very happy, I filed out with the rest of the children and Phil's mum stopped me by the door. She gave me a carrier bag full of some of Phil's old clothes. She and his dad had a way of doing these things without causing me embarrassment. They had hearts of gold.

Without James and Sam at home, I relied more and more on friends to fill the gap. One of these was Eamon. We had taken the usual route many lads take to friendship: we had a fight. It happened soon after Eamon moved into our street. We were about five at the time and sat on the grass verge in front of our houses. Our sisters were all bickering and they decided Eamon and I should have a fight to sort it out. We wrestled for ages on the floor until eventually we both just stopped and shook hands. From that day on, Eamon and I were best pals.

Hanging around with him gave me some adventures that took me away from the frightening world of my home life. We spent our days looking for ways to make a few quid here and there. We hung around the local amusement arcade scrounging fruit machine tokens from the punters. Too young to go inside (it was over-eighteens only and we were just ten or eleven), we took it in turns to run in and play our 'blagged' tokens in the machines. Any cash we won went towards buying chips and cigarettes.

We came to know where every symbol was on every reel of every machine. If a player was awarded a 'nudge' – a random feature giving them the chance to move the reels up or down to gain a win – we offered to sell them the information they needed to get a winning line for a share of their success. We raked in the 10p coins.

Although for the most part we annoyed the staff and generally made nuisances of ourselves, they looked after us once we got to know them and I've always respected them for that. They were and still are a good bunch of lads. When they weren't pissed off with us and the coast was clear, they would let us in for twenty minutes or so. Sometimes at the end of the night we cleaned the bins and swept the floor for them, earning a fiver's worth of tokens for our trouble.

Soon another interest took up most of our time: roller skating. The craze had gained new heights as Christmas arrived and we were both thrilled to get a pair of skates that year.

Now we spent our time skating around the shopping centre, car parks and outside the front of the local cinema. On Thursday nights we skated across town to the Hastings Street Roller Disco, which was held at St Mary's school hall. The small hall had a tuck shop at one end and a DJ at the other. Once he had dimmed the main lights, his disco lights turned the hall into a magical place and the beat of the music he played drummed through my body as I sped around the small wooden floor.

One such night stands out in my memory. Strutting my stuff and with my skates giving me valuable extra inches, I attracted attention. A girl approached me and told me her mate fancied me. Glad that the different colours flashing around us weren't highlighting my glowing red cheeks, I looked over to see a hippy-looking girl with long, brown hair. I liked what I saw, so I skated up to her and smiled. I took her hand and we skated around the hall. Later that night I had my first proper kiss.

When the Hastings Street Roller Disco closed down we moved to the local leisure centre on Saturday nights. Compared to St Mary's, this place was The Ritz! Music boomed around the huge space, rocking its foundations. The fantastic light show was like something from a Jean Michel Jarre concert. It was so popular they needed a bouncer just to keep the queue in order.

He was a mountain of a man whom we nicknamed 'Haystacks' as he resembled the famous wrestler of the same name.

One week in the winter, a group of kids from Nottingham came over and they were all wearing Bauer roller hockey boots covered with fur leg warmers and decorated with badges and toggles. The following week the Loughborough lot either had them on or had a pair on order, which set up a desperate longing in me to own a pair. Not holding out much hope as at £150 they were a tall order, I told my mum and then prayed and hoped for the best.

Christmas was once more upon us and during the week leading up to the big day I was on my way to roller skating when Mum stopped me at the door. "You'd better take this with you," she said, handing over £100. "I'll get the rest for you next week."

I couldn't believe it. She had been saving for weeks just so that I could get my skates on! No matter how hard times were, Mum always came through for me and I loved her to bits. I put the money down as a deposit, collected my receipt and picked out my skates. The next week dragged by, but eventually Saturday came and, true to her word, Mum gave me the other £50. I skated down to town as fast as I could and was first in the queue. Mind you, it was only half-past four and skating didn't start until seven!

I handed the man my receipt and the £50. He looked under the counter and said he had nothing for me. My heart sank, but then, looking up at me, he winked as he gave me the box with my skates inside. Phew! He was winding me up, just as he did with most kids who ordered skates from him. That night I skated more slowly than usual so that everyone could see I was the proud owner of a pair of treasured Bauer skates. I lived on

those skates for years and made many friends at the roller
disco; friends that would be around for most of my young life.

***

Soon James was on the run once again. One night he and I were
walking into town when a police car pulled up alongside us.
The officer wound his window down and shouted to us that if
we saw James we were to tell him it would be easier for him if
he turned himself in at the police station. What they really
meant was that it would be easier for them, as they didn't have
a clue where he was or how to catch him. My brother and I
played along and said, "Yes sir", and the car pulled off without
the officer realising he had just spoken to James. We laughed
our heads off and carried on into town to meet Mum.

They caught James eventually and once again moved him to a
secure unit. Being locked up and then escaping became a
constant cycle for James for a long time.

***

Sam had become a skinhead and my older brothers were all
heavily into the northern soul scene. The 'mod' revival culture
had a firm grip during the early 1980s.

Our house became more like a social club than a home once
more with people everywhere. Sam's skinhead friends hung
around there and my elder brother John had turned the back
room into a garage full of Lambretta and Vespa scooters. A few
years later he used the same space as a boxing gymnasium.

My sister Bernadette was always out clubbing or going to
northern soul all-nighters; the precursor to the rave scene. Pub
and club culture had really taken hold in my home and I hated

it. With the house full of my brothers' friends, I was stuck in the middle of disorganised chaos.

Dad continued down the path of drinking and was now always drunk. One brother was in and out of kids' homes, another was part of a skinhead gang, hell bent on causing mayhem, and my eldest brother Joseph was travelling the country snorting amphetamines off toilet seats and dancing his legs off every weekend. And besides tinkering with scooters, John terrorised our hometown with his gang of mates and a head full of violence.

Perhaps because she was fed up with everything, including her own clubbing, Bernadette eventually left. She set up home on the south coast while Helen, pregnant with the child of a local monster who treated her like shit, tried her best to play mum to me.

After a while, Dad stopped taking Mum to the pub and started going out every night on his own. Each night he got even drunker than the last and his appearance went downhill. Instead of the strong, chiselled look, he had lost weight and sported the same dirty old suit and cracked, worn-out shoes that no longer shone.

By the time Helen's baby arrived, John was in prison for fighting and Joseph and Bernadette lived away from home. Sam and James were either there or they weren't and Dad's heavy drinking resulted in a nightly ritual of shouting goodnight to every one of our neighbours and singing badly as he made his way down our street. He would stop mid-sentence and shout "I'm Sammy Skillen!" and sometimes he would hit himself in the chest and then carry on singing. I would often sit at my bedroom window watching him and wondering where my dad had gone.

The drink had truly ruined him. It was the 1980s and the Cold War was at its height; something my dad pointed out at every opportunity. When he entered the house he sat in his chair and placed his take-outs – usually two bottles of cider – down by his side and rolled himself a cigarette. Then it would start: "We're all going to die..."

Some nights I crept down the stairs and sat in the hallway that had harboured so much fun in times gone by but had become a dark, sad and lonely place for me. Trying to keep as still and quiet as I could, I would sit with tears streaming down my face, a shivering ten-year-old, wishing I could have my old dad back.

His rants started off in an informative tone, but soon shifted to loud shouting. When this happened I ran back to my bed and hid under the covers. I would pray to God like I used to with my brothers and Mum. I'd ask that the happier days would return, but they seemed to be long gone. I tried to block out the terrible visions my dad planted in my mind with his excessive shouting of the horrors that were in store for us all.

Hours went by with him saying we were all going to be killed by a Russian nuclear attack. Then Mum, unable to take anymore, would shout down the stairs telling Dad to shut up and come to bed. He would shout back: "Shut the fuck up, woman."

Like bickering children, the insults flew back and forth. Dad would remind Mum that he had "dragged her out of the gutter", and she would respond with the one line he hated the most: "Well, at least I've got a job".

This always sent Dad crazy. I believed that the loss of his job and defending my mum's and his own honour had turned him to the drink. He would stand and shout, reeling off all the places he had worked in the past and how he had spent most of his youth in a two-foot, six-inch seam digging coal, only to end up with the likes of her.

Hours went by during this exchange of insults, until eventually Dad's chest would rattle and he would start to cough. Then, just as suddenly as it had started, the arguing stopped. Dad fell to concentrating on drinking until sleep finally claimed him, leaving me a mental and physical wreck. I would sob in silent anguish until I drifted off to sleep myself.

Sometimes I would tiptoe across the landing and peek around Mum and Dad's bedroom door to see my lovely mother lying with her arm draped across her face, sobbing her heart out. As I stood, watching her weep, I wished I could take her hurt away and put back the smile that used to shine on her face as a permanent fixture.

On occasion she would catch sight of me and try to hide her anguish. Without a word she would force a teary smile and pull back the blankets. I would run over and jump into bed with her. Still silent, she would kiss me goodnight on the back of my head as I snuggled into her loving arms. Then, once more I would feel safe, though to say I was a confused child is something of an understatement!

With Mum no longer accompanying Dad to the pub, she wasn't drinking nightly, although she still had the odd Martini now and then. Despite this, she didn't quite return to her old self. Coping with Dad's drinking brought her down, but she never gave up and she got involved in many different activities with the other mothers in the street. She raised money for charity and helped organise street parties as well as spending her mornings cleaning for Mrs Ashmore.

That September, when I changed schools once more and went to De Lisle Roman Catholic High School, I stood with pride in my brand new uniform among the frightening number of kids in the playground. At that point, apart from being one of the youngest – and it goes without saying, the smallest – nothing marked me as different from any of the other 'newbies'. It was easy to see who these were; we looked about a million years younger than the second, third and fourth years with our faces scrubbed up till they shone and our clothes still bearing the crease marks of the packaging they came in.

We stood around in our respective school clans. I grouped with the lads from St Mary's and as the anticipation built I thought I stood a chance; that this could be a great turning point for me as I was no longer under the tutelage of the evil Uski. I didn't give any thought to the fact that all my brothers and sisters had attended this school and how their legacy would once more haunt me.

The morning bell rang and everyone fell silent. A parade of teachers entered the yard and stood in a row. The air was crisp and the morning dew still hung around the banks of grass that surrounded the yard. The booming voice of one of the teachers broke the silence as he instructed everyone but the first-year kids to file off into the school.

He then directed his attention to us. As he called out each of our names he sorted us into different lines. Once this was done we were led off to our classes for the day to begin.

Class was a mixture of old friends and new faces from other schools. It seemed integration between the schools was high on the agenda, as the teacher tasked us with finding out a little about each other. When it came to me, my name hung in the air, held there by a change in the teacher's demeanour. In a voice that held hostility, she asked whether I was the brother of Sam and Helen. Without thought, I proudly answered: "Yes."

"Well, let's hope you do a little bit better than they did!" she responded.

The whole class looked at me and I was embarrassed beyond belief. In that moment, all my hopes of a new beginning were dashed and I knew I was going to be clothed with the past once more and would be impacted by those who had gone before me. Without knowing it, that teacher had just broken my fucking heart!

By the third week at De Lisle, and having been the brunt of more snide comments from teachers across the school, I knew I was fighting a losing battle. I was a Skillen and the Skillens weren't liked at De Lisle. We didn't fit in.

It didn't take long for this to transmit to my fellow pupils, who thought they too could take the piss. This prompted me into the exact kind of behaviour the teachers expected of me. The first of many incidents happened as I went over to the grass banks where the school permitted us to sit during break time. Walking down the slope I passed a group of older lads playing a game with weird-looking cards that were decorated with clubs and suns.

They were getting really animated and loud, though without any nastiness. These were the Italians. Many different nationalities attended De Lisle; the only criterion was that they had to be Catholic. The main foreign groups were the Italians, the Polish and the Irish. They classed me as the latter due to my heritage.

I was walking by when suddenly I tripped over a foot that had been stuck out deliberately. I fell right down the bank. The sound of the other lads laughing at me made me feel stupid, but that emotion clouded under the anger that rose up in me at the state of my trousers. My new uniform, the best one I had ever had, was ruined. I stood up, my face burning with embarrassment and rage.

One of the Italians, a lanky lad called Ivan, stood up and asked, "Are you Sam Skillen's brother?" I told him I was, to which he replied, "Well the lad that did it was him over there". He pointed to a much older lad and added: "Sam wouldn't have stood for that."

At that, my anger turned into a seething rage. I ran over to the lad and executed a jump kick, which landed squarely in his face. His head flew back. With him off balance, the odds of his height against mine evened out and I flailed him with punches.

The Italian lads cheered me on, which encouraged me, but they also caught the attention of one of the teachers. He came running over and pulled me off the lad, then marched us both along to the headmaster's office.

Without any consultation as to why the fight had occurred, the head caned us both across the backs of our legs twice and told us to leave. On the way back to my classroom, with my legs stinging, I valiantly fought back the tears that threatened to brim over. The teacher escorting me stopped in the corridor. He looked at me and told me I had better shape up, as he had dealt with my brothers and sisters before me and would have no problem dealing with me.

The next day when I went down to the banks, Ivan the Italian – who I later learned was Ivan the Russian (how did I not click with a name like Ivan) – called me over and introduced me to the Italians, who all seemed to be called Pep!

The exception, a big guy who they called Cabbage, dealt me in to the hand of cards they were playing. The others didn't approve of this, but he said he would show me the ropes and they let it slide.

I sat with the Italian lads many a day on the banks and played cards. They accepted me into their fold and I was told by one of them that it was only because I was Irish, as the English lads had no chance of sitting in their group. The Italian lads were always good to me, especially Luciano, who would give me and Sam fruit when we were waiting for the bus outside his house.

Still not used to the ropes, I found myself singled out quite quickly and that continued. In the beginning it was humiliating and made my life a misery. The teachers at De Lisle wallowed in singling out the council estate kids for ridicule.

Take, for example, the school dinner fiasco that happened during my very early days. The teacher had been walking the queue to keep everyone in order while they waited for their dinner. There were two queues and I had been in one of them for about twenty minutes and had reached the front. The teacher on duty had spoken to me several times, so he was aware how long I had been waiting my turn. Then he approached me and asked if I was on free dinners. I don't know why he asked, because he knew that I was. I told him I was.

With a smirk of enjoyment, he said: "Well you're in the wrong queue, then."

I told him I hadn't known that there was a wrong queue and had been queuing where I was every day. His grip on my arm hurt and everyone had fallen silent. His voice boomed out as he dragged me out of line and shoved me towards the other queue.

"Back of the queue, Skillen, FREE DINNERS ARE OVER THERE!"

His smile remained constant as I made my way to the back of the free dinner queue. Those who had stood behind me a few minutes before smiled too, and others sniggered and whispered.

I hated being on free school dinners, it was without doubt modern segregation at its height. Even the dinner queue in the hall was on the opposite side from those who paid, and the food was of inferior quality. Kids that were better off took great pride in walking past the free dinner queue and taking the piss.

Shortly after this time we got a new headmaster called Mr Kennedy, who made many modern changes to the system and the kids held him in respect and liked him. But my introduction to De Lisle had set a precedent that I could not escape.

I had a few laughs, but I mostly hated it and my life outside the gates began to change and gradually took over, until eventually I stopped attending altogether. That change in my life started when James, in one of the periods when he was at home, took on the same way of dressing and started to enjoy the same music as Sam. They were also part of the same gang. The freedom they had to express themselves, uninhibited by parental interference, influenced me. I, too, had a longing to become like them: I wanted to be a skinhead.

Six

Skinheads

My desire to follow in my brothers' footsteps and be part of their music, culture and gang of friends culminated in me having my head shaved and begging my mum to get me some Doc Martens. After a few weeks of saving from her earnings, she did just that.

I thought the boots completed the overall picture, as I now dressed and looked like a skinhead. However, James and Sam informed me that there was one thing missing and they took me into the front room. A mixed feeling of excitement and wariness about what they intended to do struck me.

Sam produced a needle and a bottle of Indian ink. To become a proper skinhead I had to have a tattoo, and they did the job there and then. Not even twelve years old, I had a Doc Martens boot surrounded with the words Leicestershire Skinheads on my left arm and a fox's head with the Leicester City Football Club logo and the letters LCFC underneath on my right arm. When Mum came home she couldn't believe it, but she didn't go mad. Besides, there was nothing she could do if she had felt like doing so; it was a done deed.

I began to follow Sam everywhere, anxious to have him and the others look on me as part of the gang. They put up with me for the most part, but at night when the real game started and they went into town to find a fight with rival gangs they didn't allow me to go with them.

That changed when the annual Loughborough Fair came to town. Then they took me along and, as if it was some sort of initiation ceremony, set me off in my first proper fight, laying bets as to the outcome. Sam instructed me to go and headbutt a lad who was part of another large group. Anxious to prove myself, I did it.

I can still remember the sickening sound as the lad's nose broke and I felt his sticky wet blood clinging to me. But the encouragement of Sam and Swanny, another member of the gang, as they cheered me on for a job well done overrode those horrors. Even so, my action didn't sit well inside me and I felt bad about nutting the lad. I just knew I had to do these things to gain the approval of my brother and his gang, and if that meant I had to go against my nature to impress them, so be it.

***

By the time I had reached twelve-and-a-half years of age, I had met my own bunch of skinhead friends on the estate. We gained the nickname 'The Shelly Skins' after the name of our estate, Shelthorpe. Most of them were slightly older than me, but they accepted me as someone who was worthy of being part of the gang.

Every night we hung out at the local park until late, bantering and sometimes having the odd can of beer. It didn't seem like a big deal at the time as we all just enjoyed having a common identity.

For my thirteenth birthday we arranged to have a party at Tucker's Brickyard, a former quarry that is now a local beauty spot. Everyone saved up some cash and chipped in. We amassed a massive amount of lager and went over to the old railway bridge to what is now called Charnwood Water and drank late into the night. This was my first taste of being drunk.

I was in such a bad state they had to carry me home, where I puked my guts up before passing out.

Every night the Shelly Skins met up at the park or the local shops, and most nights we drank beer and smoked fags. That ritual altered one night when a lad called Steve brought along a can of Evo-Stik glue. He poured some into a clear, polythene bag – the kind you put your salad into at the supermarket – and started blowing in and out of the bag to inhale the fumes. It had a crazy effect on him.

Before long we all decided we wanted to try it. We went around the back of the shops and I poured the glue into the bag. As I inhaled the fumes, my ears started to buzz as if a million bees were swarming around me. My vision blurred and took me into a beautiful, dreamlike state.

Sniffing glue became a regular activity after that. Everybody had a go, but some liked it more than others. I was one of them; I wanted to sniff at every available opportunity. I loved the feeling of freedom it gave me.

Steve and I became sniffing partners for a while, but I couldn't keep up with him. He lived in a state where he was constantly off his head. Being only thirteen I had to hide my new habit from my family, as glue sniffers were the crackheads of the '80s and were looked upon with scorn by everyone.

It wasn't long, though, before it started to get the better of me and I craved the drug-induced state to the point that I skived off school to go glue sniffing with my friends. Eventually this led us all down another wrong path.

Often the only way we could get our supply of glue would be to steal it from local DIY shops. We would make our way across town to B&Q, then me and one other lad went inside the store together so that one of us could keep an eye out while the other did the deed. To complete the plan, one member of the gang waited outside the tall wire fence surrounding the outside garden area of the store, while the rest waited along the canal bank.

Once inside, we would pick one or two of the biggest cans of glue we could find, walk around the store into the open-air garden and throw it over the top of the wire to the person waiting outside. Then we would leave the store by the usual entrance as soon as we could. Getting nabbed never worried us as we never had anything on us as we left, though they did question us a few times. Whether they believed us when we said we had changed our minds about buying anything or not we never knew, but after a few weeks we returned and found they had installed a net roof over the garden department. Our raids were over.

By this point my life had a new routine. I would get up, get dressed in my tight jeans, eighteen-hole Doc Martens and denim jacket, and head out to sniff glue. In the early days of hanging around with the Shelly Skins we took turns going to each other's houses and ended up at a house of a couple of the girls we knew, whose mum we looked on as a real angel.

The girls held regular house parties and their mum welcomed us all, turning a blind eye to what we got up to. At other times we just sat around outside the shops or in the park listening to bands like The Exploited or The 4-Skins. The 'Oi!' revolution was in full swing and I loved being a part of it.

That summer's Bank Holiday Monday was a day I had looked forward to for ages. I'm not sure how it was organised, but skinheads from all over were to have a day out at the seaside, like a kind of rally. For good measure, a fight looked imminent with our rivals: the 'mods' and the 'trendies'.

When the day dawned, we met up at seven in the morning and started our journey to Skegness on the east coast, just ninety miles away. When the train pulled in it was brilliant to see that it was already packed full of skinheads from Leicester. Further up the track and the nearer we got to Skegness, the more skinheads piled on, joining at Beeston, Nottingham, Boston and Lincoln. By the time we reached our destination the train was full of skinheads shouting, singing and drinking.

Belched out onto Skegness station, we walked across the road to a massive pub on the corner. When we reached it I met a guy who wouldn't have looked out of place in a *Mad Max* film. He was massive and a tattoo of a crucified skinhead covered his back. He looked at me, smiled and said, "That's what I like to see. Start 'em young!" His beautiful girlfriend, who had feather-cut hair, came over and cuddled me, and pride swelled in my chest. I felt I was part of the gang and her boyfriend was obviously the leader, so I thought I could do anything.

I pushed my way through skinheads and punks of all shapes and sizes and headed for the bar. I asked the barman for a pint of lager, even though I was thirteen years old and looked about ten. The barman surveyed me up and down and then, without questioning me, he pulled my pint.

I couldn't believe it. It was my first ever time in a pub without my parents and was definitely the first time I had ever bought an alcoholic drink for myself. When I turned to walk out I felt like I had just conquered Everest. Standing right behind me was the warrior skinhead. He winked at me, then looked knowingly across at the barman. I winked back and made my way outside.

After spending a while in the pub like an army ready for battle, we headed for the seafront, chanting as we marched. Being young and still not yet wise to the ways of the world, I didn't understand the undertones of what was really going on. The battle cry was "Sieg Heil!" and I shouted it as loud as any of the others as we followed behind the warrior skinhead.

I soon found out that this wasn't just some ordinary day out at the beach for a bunch of likeminded kids; this was the real thing, instigated by the National Front. And trouble was about to flare up.

We made our way into a car park near the seafront, and as we walked across it I saw a few Asian families about to enjoy a day out at the beach. Without warning, the warrior skinhead shouted, "Paki bastards!" This set the tone for the whole group.

There must have been two hundred or more skinheads taunting those poor families. I felt sorry for them and wanted to get out of there. But before I could move, over the sand dunes came our arch enemies: around a hundred mods and trendies; football hooligans wearing the latest designer clothes. They picked up rocks and started pelting us.

The sound of glass splintering as car windscreens smashed around us was matched only by the creaks and bangs of roofs and bonnets taking direct hits and denting under the pressure. Into this mix, the screams and insults that cut across the air turned the car park into a battlefield. Rocks the size of tennis balls and bigger hurled back and forth until one of the skinhead girls fell to her knees. Her face was split open and blood was pouring onto the tarmac. The hatred spilled over and we charged towards our foe. They met us halfway.

The arrival of the police saw us all adopt one common goal: to get the hell out of there. Everybody ran towards the centre of Skegness, where we skinheads regrouped on a street corner. Across the road a group of mods sat on their shiny scooters. The passion of our hatred drove us to run at them. We got one off his scooter and kicked him half to death. Satisfied that we had done a good job, we left them and made our way into the town centre. Here we sat on the roof of the public toilets, chanting.

Swelled in number by a snatch squad, the police surrounded us. This elite force infiltrated the crowd, dragging known faces out and arresting them. When they took my friend Steve I ran at the copper responsible, kicking and punching him. He lifted me up like a rag doll and threw me into the back of an already overcrowded Black Maria. Unable to get up, I lay on the floor gasping for air beneath dozens of Doc Martens. One of the older lads dragged me out of the pile and I sat next to him. He winked and said, "Good lad."

I didn't answer. Nicked for the first time ever, I was shitting myself. Up my sleeve I had a half-sniffed bag of glue I had used in the toilet on the train. I had to get rid of it.

Made for bigger wrists than mine, the handcuffs allowed me some movement. I managed to wriggle my arms until the glue bag fell onto the seat behind me.

When we arrived at the police station the back doors opened and the police filed us out one at a time. The 'winker' stood up and there was my glue bag on the seat next to him. 'Fuck,' I thought, 'I am in so much shit.'

The copper saw the bag, picked it up and examined it. Then he turned to the winker and punched him full in the face. "You dirty bastard," he said and dragged him into the station. Relief filled me and I felt glad that I hadn't born the brunt of the copper's knuckles.

Inside the station they removed our boots and put us straight into cold cells. Reality kicked in; this was no game. The dread inside me clutched at my stomach muscles.

After a time, an officer came. He took me out of the cell and up to the large counter, which looked a lot like the bar in the pub I had stood at a few hours earlier. The desk sergeant looked me up and down and frowned. "How old are you, son?" he asked.

I told him my age and his face turned to shock. He asked me who I was with and, not wanting to grass on Steve, I told him I was on my own. After a few more questions they led me to another cell without any other prisoners in it. This cell had a wooden bed running along one side and a steel toilet in the corner. I wrapped myself up in the dirty green blanket that was on the bed (which had more holes than it had fabric) and tried to get warm.

Eventually I fell asleep. It was Steve that woke me as they had put him in the same cell. We laughed at each other and then Steve produced a bag of glue and started sniffing. I couldn't believe that even locked in a police cell Steve was still sniffing glue!

When we awoke in the morning the cell door opened and a

copper brought us each a cup of tea and an egg sandwich. The sandwich tasted horrible, so I just drank the tea, but Steve was starving so he ate mine as well. This didn't bother me. Going without was the norm for me; I was used to the feeling of hunger.

We didn't have long to wait after that as the copper came back and took us back to the large counter. The desk sergeant gave us our boots and a piece of paper informing us that we had to appear at Skegness Magistrates' Court in a month's time. Then they released us.

So there we were in the middle of Skegness with fuck all money and no way of getting home. I was expecting my parents to be waiting, but nobody came. With the small amount of change Steve had in his pocket we caught a train and planned to stay on it all the way back to Loughborough, but we were kicked off at Boston because they caught Steve sniffing from his bag of glue. To this day I do not know how he managed to keep that hidden from the coppers!

The day was hot and sticky and we had no other choice but to start walking. I was scared and tired of acting like the tough guy. I just wanted to be back at home in the arms of my mum.

We walked for hours until thirst forced me to approach one of the expensive-looking bungalows that lined the road. I asked a lady for some water. She went into her house and returned with a milk bottle filled with cold water. I thanked her and took the water with me. As we headed off along the road, darkness started to close in. Steve talked about sleeping in the hedgerow, but I didn't like the sound of that because of my fear of the dark.

Without a care in the world, Steve started sniffing from his bag of glue again. Tears pricked the back of my eyes. It took me my entire muster not to cry. I remember clasping my hands together and praying to God to somehow get me home. I had a dread of spending the night outside and alone in the dark.

As if in answer to my prayers, a Schepens and Wells removal lorry passed us. This was a well-known Loughborough removal company. I couldn't believe my eyes and wished we could have stopped it. Then, in the distance, we did see it stop. I grabbed Steve and told him to put his glue bag away. As we approached the lorry, the door opened and the driver leaned out and asked us if we needed a lift. I said yes and we jumped in.

To his question about where we were headed, I told him, "Loughborough."

He smiled and said: "It's your lucky day, lads, because so am I."

The tiredness in my body had dulled my wit, so I didn't even flinch at him stating the obvious. After about ten minutes he turned, looked me in the eye and said, "Do you believe in God, son?"

His words seemed like some kind of sign, as just a short time earlier I had been on the verge of tears and desperately praying, and now here I was in the cab of a truck with the driver asking me if I believed in God. It was weird, but I said: "Yeah, I think I do now."

The truck driver smiled and replied: "Well I do, too, and that's why I stopped. I'm a volunteer for the Salvation Army at weekends."

I felt comfortable in the company of this man and when we got back to Loughborough I thanked him and promised him I would visit the Salvation Army one day. Little did I know how that promise would one day come to pass!

My brothers saw me coming as I arrived at the end of Manor Drive. All I wanted was for someone to be concerned, someone to have missed me. I was confused as to why nobody had come to fetch me from Skegness police station. I put on a brave face, but inside I was crying. I approached our house to the sound of my brothers clapping and Mum calling out from the open bedroom window, "You made it, then?"

A niggle of anger clenched me as I looked up at her and the thought went through my head: '*Yeah, I made it, but where were you?!*'

I returned to Skegness to face the magistrates a few weeks later. This time I had Mum and our social worker with me. I received a Supervision Order, which meant I had to report to a social worker once a week, and on top of this I was given a fine of £15.

Seven

Nightmares Revisited

Shortly after my Skegness adventure I went down to the local shops to meet up with the rest of the gang, but nobody was around. I sat down on the wall and waited. After a while, a fat kid who wasn't one of the regulars turned up. He had a tin of glue. This was enough to tempt me into spending time in his company.

We went over to the small quarry next to the nearby church and prepared a couple of bags to sniff. He poured loads of glue into my bag and within minutes I was out of it. Through the haze of nothingness swimming in my head, I had an awareness that my body had landed in some bushes. I opened my eyes. For a moment I wondered if what I saw was real or if my hallucination had brought back the worst moment of my life.

My mind couldn't accept that it was happening again, but it was. The fat kid was stood over me with his dick out, trying to force himself on me! I froze, unable to think straight or to fight him off. At that moment, like a voice from heaven – though I doubt any angel would swear like it – I heard Andy, one of the Shelly Skins, shout, "You dirty bastard!" The fat kid's body then overbalanced, helped by a shove from Andy.

I was already a member of the gang, but they all particularly looked out for me due to me being much smaller than the rest of them. And on that day I really needed this extra help. More concerned for me than my would-be rapist, Andy took no notice of the fat kid making his exit, but set about bringing me back to my senses.

Once I felt alright, Andy took me to where he knew the fat kid would be. I armed myself with a scaffolding pole. I had to show him and any others that they couldn't mess with me, despite my size, and that getting me on my own wasn't a licence to take the piss.

When we came up to him my size held no meaning. The humiliation and hurt I had suffered came to the fore and I swung violently at him. I knew inside that I could have bashed his head in, but he ran away. Fear was now gripping *him*. I could hear my own voice, like that of someone possessed, as I shouted after him, calling him a nonce.

I had the satisfaction of everyone knowing what he had tried to do, but I hated him for doing that to me. And even though I had had some kind of revenge, the incident triggered the return of the nightmares.

A few years later I learned that the fat kid had been found dead in his own home. He had committed suicide. A part of me thought then that his demons must have been bigger than mine for him to have lost the will to carry on living.

My elder brother John put paid to my glue-sniffing era. Just out of prison, he caught me one night in a telephone phone box with my nose in a bag. All it took was for someone to care. His kind of tough love scared the shit out of me, but it did the trick. He grabbed me, held me tightly by the arms and told me that if he ever caught me sniffing glue again he would batter me. I went home that night and never picked up the glue again.

I carried on hanging about with the Shelly Skins for a while until, one Thursday night, something I saw and heard on *Top of the Pops* had such a profound effect on me that it changed my life forever.

All the usual stuff came on – the bands and singers of the day – and then the presenter introduced a new group called Break Machine. They played their "Street Dance" number and danced in a way that I had never seen before, mimicking the movements of a robot. They moonwalked across the stage and finally spun around on their backs and their heads. It was magical.

I stood up and tried to copy these moves. There I was, in full skinhead garb and sporting a mohican, trying to moonwalk across my front room.

The next day with my skinhead mates all I could think about was the dancers from the night before. Over the following weeks more and more songs and dance music hit the radio stations and television screens. I was witnessing the birth of breakdance in the UK and it didn't take long for me to ditch the skinhead look for baggy jeans and trainers. My new haunt at this time was the town centre. Here I made new friends and one of them, Wayne, took me to the barbers to have my mohican shaved off. My skinhead days were over.

It's a funny thing for a fourteen-year-old to say, but that was my life. My childhood hadn't lasted long, and at this still very young age I had experienced stuff I should never have come across and was now ready to move on.

Eamon and I started to hang out together again as he was never interested in the skinhead culture and for a few years we had gone our separate ways. But at this point we rekindled our friendship.

The local cinema had installed a small arcade of video games and two pool tables. A tall, grey-haired man named Mr Spary, who wouldn't have looked out of place playing a general in a First World War movie, ran the cinema with military precision. A lot of the kids thought he was too strict, but he was always kind to me and I respected him. After he left, Brenda, a red-haired lady, took over. She immediately ordered more video games and the place became a hotspot for teenagers. It was busy every night of the week and packed on a Saturday afternoon.

For 10p a go you could play a classic video game, such as *Space Invaders*, *Defender*, *Galaxian* or *Donkey Kong* for ten or twenty minutes, depending on how good you were. Some of us played them so often we could stay on for half an hour. One lad named Greg became the video game king.

Tall and skinny, Greg was into heavy metal music, and he dressed and wore his hair accordingly. His game was *Galaxian* and when he took his seat in front of the table-top game, people would gather round to watch. Any normal player would score around fifty thousand points and clear ten to fifteen sheets on this game, but Greg was different and it was not unusual for us to go around town, come back an hour later and find him still playing the same game!

Sure enough, Eamon and I soon worked out a scam. We would 'strim' a machine using a length of plastic cable with a hook on one end to reach into the machine's coin mechanism and register free game credits.

We made our money by selling these credits at two for the price of one. Brenda eventually worked out why her takings had fallen so much and getting caught strimming resulted in a three-month ban from both the arcade and the cinema. But Brenda had a heart of gold and she let us back in after a week or so, only for us to let her down by doing the same thing again.

The cinema had a half-price ticket night on Monday evenings and every kid in Loughborough turned up to take advantage of this cheap offer. The queues often stretched out the doors and down to the town hall some two hundred yards away.

Without a doubt, one of the most unforgettable Monday night movies for me was *Breakdance: The Movie*. Every kid in the land had seen Break Machine on *Top of the Pops* and the British breakdancing scene had exploded. On the night the movie was shown, kids wearing baseball caps and either tracksuit bottoms or baggy jeans packed the cinema.

Popcorn flew, the sound of Slush Puppies being slurped filled the air and many a lad was busy getting a 'stinky pinky' in the back row! The film started and the sounds of early hip hop and breakbeat filled the auditorium. We all went wild, dancing in our seats, body popping in the aisles and even jumping up onto the stage and breakdancing beneath the screen. One of the film's main characters danced with a broom to the sound of Kraftwerk and the place erupted even more.

From that night on we found a new haunt and the place to be was 'the hut'; a non-descript shelter alongside the bowling greens and toilets in the town's Queen's Park. Day in and day out, a group of us would hang around in the hut breakdancing. Bassett, one of the lads, brought his massive, portable ghettoblaster with him and we practised our moves for hours on end.

I wasn't brilliant, but I loved the music and felt I was part of the gang. Something akin to happiness stayed with me during this time in my life as I spent my days and nights doing what I loved: roller skating back at the leisure centre, playing video games, watching movies or just breakdancing in the park.

Eight

The Raid

Dad's drunken rants had become part of the routine of home life and didn't bother me as much as they had once done. At fifteen and coping well I found I no longer disliked him; I just felt sorry for him.

'Home' merely represented the house we lived in rather than the cosy place the word usually conjures up. It still burst at the seams with my brothers' friends and Sam and James were around more often. Helen had had two babies with the monster by this time and Joseph was back in town. Bernadette hadn't returned. She continued to carve out a life for herself on the south coast.

The scooter scene was massive. The older lads in the area, including John and Sam, had amassed an impressive collection of Lambrettas and Vespas. Every lad who needed his scooter fixing came to them. Scooter rallies became the new 'in' thing and, according to the tales my brothers told on their return, were just another breeding ground for fights and running battles with the police.

The reputation John and Sam had created for themselves around the town for starting and getting involved in fights inevitably impacted on me.

I would hear people say: "That's one of the Skillens." Our family name had become notorious, and was instantly associated with violence. I faced challenges along the lines of, "You think you're hard because you're a Skillen", or "Just because your brothers are tough, it don't mean that you are". To be honest, I couldn't give a fuck either way at first, but after a time I got sick of the comments and started lashing out.

In the end, I found that I also had a taste for it. I became a bully on the back of my brothers' reputation. They had quite a few people in fear and I played on it. I wasn't the best fighter, but I had a lot of bottle and would have a go even though lack of good nutrition as a child meant that almost every other kid was bigger than me. I ragged people up for their dinner money or robbed them of their bus fare. Secretly, I didn't like the person that I was becoming and one day I got the comeuppance I deserved.

It happened while I was out with Eamon. We spotted a small, blond-haired kid with his little brother. I went over and asked him for money and he refused to hand it over. I told him he had better give me his money or I would batter him. He pushed his little brother behind him and stood firm. I had never encountered this before and it scared me. I fed him the old bully line, telling him that the next time I saw him I would beat him up. He just stood there and asked me what was wrong with sorting it out here and now.

My heart fell out of my arse. I had never experienced this response before. What did I do? I bottled it. I turned and ran away. That incident marked the end of my career as a bully, but I've never forgotten that kid. He taught me a valuable lesson; one I would use for my own gains later in life.

***

Hanging around with my friends outside the Curzon Cinema one night, the conversation turned to a bloke we had seen jump from the Carillon Tower and War Memorial in the centre of

Queen's Park. At the time, a few of us had been in the hut looking towards the memorial – a huge tower – when Mason, one of the lads, noticed a man climbing over the fencing at the top. The next thing we knew he had jumped and a massive thud followed as he hit the ground. It was a fall of a hundred feet or so.

We ran over, but there was nothing we could do. He looked stone dead. Mason covered him with his coat and someone ran to telephone an ambulance and the police. When they arrived they asked us a few questions and it was these questions we were discussing outside the cinema when a man came over and started ranting at us. He had known the dead man and said that we should have more respect. But we weren't being disrespectful, we were just talking about what we had witnessed. He became irate and started shouting.

The cinema is in the very centre of Loughborough, so it was no great surprise when my eldest brother Joseph and a few of his friends arrived on the scene. Joseph spoke to the angry man, who then left us alone. Joseph told us that if we needed him he would be in a nearby pub. With the drama over, most of the other kids went home, but I decided to go and see Joseph in the pub.

As I got near the doors, Joseph came out, and what followed shocked me. Two men grabbed Joseph and then my brothers John and Sam appeared as if from nowhere. John pulled one of the men off Joseph and asked him what he was doing. Joseph took his chance, broke free and ran off.

John let go of the man when he produced his police identity card. The two coppers didn't hang around; they chased after Joseph and caught him down a nearby alleyway.

Still in awe of it all, I felt Sam press a tin into my hand. He looked at me and said, "Leg it!" Without hesitation, I stuffed the tin down my trousers and ran as fast as I could towards home. Once out of sight I stopped and looked inside the tin. It was full of white powder wrapped in paper. It turned out to be amphetamines.

When I got home, my brothers were clearing stuff out of the house and hiding it across the road in Andy's back garden. Then we waited for the inevitable: for the coppers to start bashing at our door. My stomach rolled over with nerves; I was scared shitless.

It was the drug squad, and this was what they called a raid. They searched everywhere but found nothing. Because of my young age they allowed me to leave, so I went to Helen's house up the road. If they had searched me they would have found the evidence they needed, but luckily for me and everyone else, they didn't.

Nine

A Member of the Night Club

John's reputation around the town was huge and he had started working as doorman at a nightclub called Sammy's. I took to hanging around outside the front before it got busy, talking to him and the other doormen. Bill, one of the managers, would send me to the chippy or to Pete's burger van to get him a snack. One night the club was really busy and I was asked to help out in the cloakroom. This was how my introduction to the nightlife of Loughborough began.

I knew Darren, one of the other younger lads who worked there, as we had grown up on the same street. His beautiful sister Michelle was my first ever girlfriend when I was around five years old! Darren showed me the ropes and we worked away happily all night. The place set me buzzing and I really loved working there.

There were two rules we had to follow – no drinking and no going upstairs – but Darren found a way around this and it was the manager Bill, a big guy with a legendary drinking habit, who unwittingly provided it.

It wasn't unusual for Bill to sink ten pints of lager before work and another dozen while he was actually at work, but the weird thing was that it never seemed to affect him. At regular intervals he called Darren over and told him to run upstairs and get him a 'lager top'. It was always the same, he never asked for anything different. Darren took the opportunity to ask Bill if we could have a drink, knowing that the answer would be "soft drinks only".

The drinks Darren brought down for us appeared to be lemonade, but they had a hidden secret: the lemonade was mixed with white wine. Throughout the night, many requests came from Bill and each time he would allow us our 'soft drink'. Darren and I turned into happy drunks as we worked.

Not going upstairs changed for me one night when, with the club throbbing with customers, Darren had to help collect glasses, leaving me to run the cloakroom. At one point the queue had dwindled to nothing, and over the loud music Bill shouted, "Oi! Dickhead!" (he had a way with words). He tossed his pint glass to me and said "lager top". The lads on the door just laughed at my new nickname and I walked upstairs, not knowing what to expect. I opened the double doors at the entrance to the disco and the music hit me like a train. Wow! The dry ice, the disco lights, the girls… it was intoxicating.

I weaved my way through the crowd and down past the pool table to the bottom bar. The bar tender, Rob, stood at the side of the bar. For a moment memories flooded back to me as I looked at him. He was immaculate in a white shirt with a black bow tie and trousers, with his shoes shining and not a hair out of place. I thought of my dad before the demon drink had seduced him.

Rob not only looked the part, he was the coolest barman I had ever seen. When he went behind the bar to get my order he did so like a skater might on ice and even managed to make pouring a lager top look cool. Without me asking for it, he took another glass and filled it with white wine and lemonade, then floated back to where I stood and put the drinks on the bar. I picked up the lager to take it to Bill. "Don't forget yours," Rob shouted, winking at me.

Rob was Darren's link to the bar, and now I had made contact. I felt fantastic. As I walked through the crowd I looked over and saw the DJ conducting a crowd of people who were sitting on the floor in rows. They swayed from side to side to the sound of "Oops Upside Your Head", a massive late '70s and early '80s dance hit for The Gap Band.

This idyllic scene of a happy, carefree crowd having a good time suddenly erupted in front of me as a shaven-headed lad butted another lad and a brawl broke out. The doormen were there within seconds, wading in and knocking lads out left, right and centre.

There were no questions asked, just an outburst of violence that ended with punters sprawled across the floor. They were then dragged by their feet down the steep flight of stairs and thrown out into the street. Sammy's had a reputation for violence and this was the first time I had witnessed it. But this reputation was well-deserved.

I worked in the cloakroom at Sammy's six nights a week for £10 per shift and a few staff 'lemonades' until one night the general manager, John, gave me a dickie bow. He told me to wear black and whites the next night as I would be working upstairs. I was made up. The next day I went out and got myself some black trousers and a smart white shirt. Darren and I worked collecting glasses at a rate of knots. The club heaved to well over capacity with students and the bars were always five or six deep with punters.

Desperate to impress, I rushed around the club stacking glasses ten high, winding my way back and forth through the crowd from the glass washing machine. Then Rob stopped me and pulled me to one side. He told me to slow down and take it easy or I would put people out of a job. I was making it look like we only needed one glass collector, when we actually had four. "The secret," said Rob, "is to pace yourself." This was the first of many lessons learned that day.

The staff soon introduced me to the 'Curzon Hotel'. Sammy's and the town's cinema were attached, and next to the bottom bar, hidden behind red velvet curtains, was a fire exit. This led directly into the cinema's upper foyer. One night Rob and Darren and a few of the doormen were stood with their heads poking through the curtains, giggling like kids.

Intrigued by this, I didn't hesitate when Rob called me over and pulled back one of the curtains. I peeked around the door. There stood one of the doormen leaning against the wall getting a blowjob from one of the local girls. With her back towards us, she didn't know we were watching.

The doorman kept giving us the thumbs-up, and as our sniggers got louder the girl realised we were watching and laughing. I thought she would go mental, but she just raised her hand and waved. We all cheered and let her finish the job!

At the end of that night we all sat and had a staff drink. Rob poured me a white wine and lemonade right in front of Bill. I looked at Bill and he said: "What are you waiting for, dickhead? It's not as if you ain't had one before!"

I loved Bill and his straight up way of putting things. I laughed and downed my wine. Working at Sammy's, Darren and I became like brothers and on our nights off we hit the town together.

I never had much money, but Darren worked as a builder during the daytime and often paid for my nights out. Small in height but with the physique of a professional boxer, he could fight like fuck and had a fiery nature. In a town known for its violence, this combination meant we always ended up in a brawl.

Too small to be tough, I had been taking kickboxing lessons and trained at the local boxing club, but it was nothing major, not like Darren. He was an expert at this level, so my nightly routine during this period of my life was work, drink, fight, work, drink, fight. But then again, in our neck of the woods, this was the norm for most lads of my age.

***

When I wasn't working, and as I was now nearly a man (or so I thought at 17 years old), my friends and I had graduated from the cinema and we all hung around in a new wine bar called Next Door.

Wine bars became the big thing in the mid '80s and, although small, this was the best our town had to offer. We would meet up outside The Casablanca, Loughborough's busiest pub. As you might guess, it was next door to the wine bar, which had its own disco and dance floor. It heaved with punters from opening until closing time, and almost all of the people who drank there were underage. Getting inside never posed a problem for me as I knew all the doormen from Sammy's.

One night I spotted a local girl in the bar. Considered by my mates to be the best looking girl in town, her boyfriend was a handsome beggar too! They looked like a model couple and I thought I had no choice but to admire her from afar. Later that night at Sammy's, a little bird told me she had parted company with her boyfriend. So being the cheeky chap I am, I took it upon myself to buy her a drink. She stood with a friend in the 'speakeasy'; a quiet bar area in the club used by couples for a kiss and a cuddle and, on the odd occasion, much more!

My nerves jangled as I approached her for a few reasons. First, I thought I had no chance. Second, she was beautiful and well out of my league. Third, she was standing with a group of friends who were also all beautiful.

I steeled myself to go over and ask her if she wanted a drink. And she said yes! Stunned, I bought her a drink and got myself the usual white wine and lemonade. We chatted, laughed and joked until her model boyfriend returned and rudely interrupted us. The little bird had lied.

He walked straight up and put his arms around her to let me know I was very much on his patch. I just looked him up and down and laughed. She smiled sweetly at me and followed him out of the club. He looked back at me and winked as they left, the smug bastard. But what he didn't know was that she had done the same. One nil!

The next week, the beauty came back to the club. I had been looking forward to seeing her all week long, and here she was standing in front of me, arguing with her boyfriend. I wanted to go over and punch his smug face, but I thought better of it.

Later that night he made the decision for me. He thought it would be a good idea to warn me off his girlfriend and I thought it would be a good idea to smack him on the jaw. So I did. Two nil.

At the end of the night, and to everyone's amazement (including my own), I left the club with the girl of my dreams on my arm. Three nil and game over.

After that night I spent every night with her. It was a true love story. She was from the posh side of town and I was from the rough end. Her mum hated her going out with me as I represented everything a mother wouldn't want for her daughter. I knew I was a victim of my family's reputation, and deep inside I hated that fact.

We did what most of you reading this have done at one time or another. We stayed indoors watching videos, eating Chinese food, drinking wine and falling in love. As time went by, my feelings for her became so strong they took control over my common sense and the green-eyed monster worked its way into my mind.

Instead of being proud of my beautiful girlfriend, I hated it when other lads looked at her or spoke to her. It filled me with jealous rage and I ended up fighting with lads and arguing with her. This went on for months until eventually she went on holiday with her friends and didn't come back. I was heartbroken. I hadn't lost her, I had driven her away.

Ten

The 'Trip' of a Lifetime

By the time I turned nineteen, drugs were nothing new to me. At fourteen Joseph had taken me to my first northern soul all-nighter. He and his mate Baggy Dave – they called him that due to the thirty-two-inch flared trousers he used to wear – took me into the toilets and I watched as they snorted speed (amphetamines) off the toilet cistern.

I knew what it was as my brothers and their mates were always talking about it and I had seen them passing it around. After a whispered chat they laid out a small line and offered it to me. I took the rolled up £5 note from Joseph and snorted the line. It stung my nostrils and the bitter taste hit the back of my throat, making me gag.

Dave and Joe laughed and led me out into the dance hall. The music was loud and after a while things started to look more vivid than normal. A rush of energy surged through me from my feet to the tip of my nose. I felt so alive. I started dancing to the sounds of Edwin Starr's "Twenty-Five Miles" and didn't stop until three hours later. People shook my hand and complimented me on my dancing. That was my first drug-induced high, and for that one night I never once felt the fear that had followed me around since the loss of my innocence.

This experience wasn't a one-off, as a few weeks after my northern soul adventure with Joe, a friend and I met a punk rocker named Clive. He asked us if we fancied a smoke. We had often nicked the odd Park Drive off my Dad or a Player's No. 6 from Mum's handbag, so I thought, why not?

We went around the back of the local Kwik Save and sat down next to the small canal. Clive took out a packet of Rizla papers and stuck them together to make one large cigarette paper. He filled it with tobacco, then took out a large brown lump that looked like liquorice.

I hadn't clicked on until this point that the 'smoke' he referred to was of the Moroccan variety. We watched as he held his Clipper lighter underneath the large piece of hash and warmed it. The aroma filled my nostrils as he crumbled it into the large reefer he had built and then held the newly crafted joint up and admired his own handiwork.

When he lit it blue, sweet-smelling smoke filled the air. He passed it to me. I held it in my mouth and drew on it. The smoke filled my lungs and made me cough. Clive laughed and said, "Hold it down." I drew again and this time held the smoke down for as long as I could. My friend went next. I watched as he drew in deep on the joint a few times and then passed it back to Clive.

As we walked into town a little later I didn't feel anything at first, but the further we walked the more relaxed I felt. By the time we entered the shopping centre it had hit me. I looked at my friend and he started to giggle. This set me off. Then Clive started to giggle and that was it; we were crying with laughter like a pack of hyenas.

People must have thought we were crazy. The laughing lasted for about half an hour, and then my mouth became so dry that my tongue started to stick to the roof of my mouth. I went into the newsagent's on the corner, gulped a bottle of orange straight down and stood in the queue waiting to pay for the empty bottle. When I reached the counter I had forgotten why I was there. I stood there looking at the empty bottle, then at the woman at the till, not knowing what to do.

I just walked out of the shop and nobody said a word. Clive and my friend had been watching through the window and were literally rolling on the floor with laughter, but I was still dazed and confused.

My thirst had subsided, but I then had the most amazing urge to eat. The 'munchies' had got me. The other two went into a local supermarket while I sat, zombie-like, on a bench. They came out a few minutes later with crisps and chocolate. We sat and ate for what seemed like an eternity and I had never tasted anything so good!

***

By the time acid house exploded onto the scene between 1989 and early 1990, my experiences in the drug-taking game had equipped me to try anything.

Smiley t-shirts and headscarves were the fashion statement of the day and the *ITV News at Ten* reported on the acid house scene in London. Early hip hop had progressed and the DJs from New York's club scene had created a sound that spread around the world like wildfire.

I was at a low point in my life at this time and needed a lift, so a friend and I decided to drop some acid. We wanted to experience the mind-bending effect we had heard it had, so we gave it a try.

I knew a local hippy who was notorious for his drug taking and a good bet as a source for acid. When we went round to see him he gave me four orange squares that looked like small postage stamps, with a small black circle on each one.

The hippy told me they weren't too strong, so we should take two each to guarantee a "decent trip". Well, he knew best! This hippy had an infamous reputation among hardened drug takers for his capacity to handle 'hard' drugs and so, on reflection, I should have taken this into consideration, as the "decent trip" I had is something I will never forget!

We dropped the acid, two each like he said, and walked into town. About twenty minutes later my friend asked me if I felt anything and, at that stage, neither of us had. We continued to walk into Queen's Park, where just a few years earlier we had frequently breakdanced.

Walking ahead of my friend I suddenly realised things looked a bit different. The pale blue sky of the hot summer's evening turned purple and then green. And before long it shone with all the colours of the rainbow. Wow, the acid had kicked in.

I turned to speak to my friend, but he was no longer just behind me. He stood on the other side of the park, staring at me. "Pete," he shouted, "how are you doing that?" I looked across at him, puzzled. "You're floating above the water!" he yelled.

It was crazy. He kept shouting and laughing, while pointing at me and repeating himself. The next thing I remember, my friend and I were sitting under a bush rubbing our faces and hair with soil and talking about getting camouflaged so that "they" couldn't find us. To this day I don't have a clue who "they" were.

Eventually we came out of the bushes and back into an alternate reality. Our faces were black with dirt. My friend panicked and said he had to get home. We walked for what felt like hours surrounded by all manner of things. Vivid colours encircled us and the heat of the sun made me think I was in a desert.

A Harley Davidson motorbike passed us as we walked down the newly built bypass towards Shelthorpe. The roar of the engine sounded like the growl of a great beast and the long hair poking out the bottom of the rider's helmet seemed to stretch out into the air twenty feet behind him. He looked at me and smiled as he passed, as if he knew I was tripping. This sent us into a state of total paranoia.

My friend wanted to go to the local cemetery, stating that it was his time to die. This happy trip had turned into a hellish nightmare. Every person we saw had a massive head and staring eyes that leered at us. I was petrified, and all my worst dreams were becoming a reality. I walked into the house and saw my dad sitting on the sofa having one of his rare sober moments. I sat down next to him and looked at my feet. They were starting to melt. I told Dad that my legs were falling off and my feet were melting. I began to cry.

He fetched my mum, who bungled me into the next-door neighbour's car to take me to hospital. At that moment John arrived in his van and took charge of the situation.

He took me from the car to his van, where he sat me next to his new girlfriend on the front seat. John explained that I needed something to help bring me down from my nightmare trip. A sense of calm came over me as I listened to him.

He drove us to the local fish and chip shop, and as he went inside to buy orange juice and food I watched him through a windscreen that I thought was made of water.

I reached out to touch it. At that moment, nausea waved over me and I threw up out of the side window. I climbed over the seats and into the back of the old Sherpa van. John's girlfriend watched me, her expression half amused and half freaked out.

I ended up staying with my big brother and sleeping on a mattress next to his bed. He looked after me through the night as the trip slowly wound down.

They found my friend the next day asleep on a grave in the cemetery and he has never been the same since. He continued to experiment more and more with acid, but for me that was the first and last time in my life. I had learned the hard way that drugs were not for me.

Over the following months, holed up in my bedroom listening to Jeff Wayne's *Musical Version of the War of the Worlds* – a surreal experience in itself – I experienced vivid dreams, suffered panic attacks and would slip back into my nightmare trip. I have since learned that these are secondary hallucinations and can continue for years. In my case, they did.

Eleven

A New Love

My new girlfriend Emma came into my life while I was still only nineteen. She was two years younger than me, but our attraction to and feelings for each other were very strong. The only problem was her dad, who hated me from day one.

Within a few months of us becoming a couple, Emma fell pregnant and we moved into my family's house. We had nothing, and the thought of bringing a baby into the world frightened me. We were both still kids ourselves.

Not long after Emma and I met, Sammy's Nightclub closed down. Along with the rest of the staff I went to work for two local businessmen who had bought Mr Christopher's, a cabaret club. After a massive revamp that turned the place into a modern nightclub, they changed the name to Crystals.

Right from the start this venue buzzed. I worked as a barman and without me realising it at first, my drinking increased to more than just a few with my mates or the odd one while I worked. It was not uncommon for me to have eight or nine pints of lager washed down with a couple of chasers during my nightly shift behind the bar. I could hold my drink well and, although pissed out of my head by the end of the night, I appeared as straight as a die to anyone I spoke to.

As my family home was unsuitable for us we moved into bed and breakfast accommodation with several other families. Our 'home' was a tiny single room while we waited for the local council to house us.

But even though Emma was heavily pregnant with our first

child, I still wasn't around. I was at work, and if I wasn't working I'd be at The Bitter End. This was the busiest pub in town due to the fact that the DJ, Jez Dennett, was the only guy in town playing rave music. I behaved as if I was still single and still the lad about town, meeting up with my friends, getting drunk and usually ending up fighting.

To my shame, I remember one particular Friday night when I went out to get some milk so that Emma and I could drink a pot of tea. I headed towards town, intending to have a quick pint in the pub and pick up the milk on the way back home.

I entered The Bitter End and met up with an old friend, Adi. We ordered a drink and noticed that a few lads were giving Jez hassle. They had asked for rock music and Jez had refused to play it. Carmel, the pub's landlady, had gone to sort it out. One of these lads squared up to Carmel, so I stepped forward and told the lad to leave it out.

One of his mates stepped towards me and I hit him straight on the button. Down he went like a sack of shit and I stamped on his face three times before the rest of them could move a muscle. Not that it mattered when they did, as Adi knocked them both out with one punch each. I drew on my cigarette, lent over the lad I had put away and stubbed it out in his eye.

We left The Bitter End, went off into town and headed to the coast for a weekend rave we had heard was taking place in Skegness. A voice inside me told me that this was wrong, but I went along anyway without a thought for Emma and our unborn baby. She never did get her cup of tea and had to borrow money to survive the weekend, but instead of dropping me like she should have, she listened to my pathetic excuses and shallow promises and forgave me.

***

A few weeks later, the council allocated us a council flat in the Russell Street area of Loughborough. We knew we were going to a shithole of an estate, but we made the best of it. It was our first proper home and after my upbringing on the roughest estate in town it felt like a holiday camp to me. We moved in and I decorated as well as I could.

Emma went into labour with our first child on a Sunday and Jade was born on January 13, 1991. I was present for the birth and proud to be a father. I cried like a baby when Jade arrived, overcome by how beautiful she was. I sat and looked at Emma with our child in her arms and promised her that I would try harder to be better.

I made my way back to our third floor flat, sat down and vowed that I would not let Emma or my new daughter down. The time for me to change had come. But as I sat there making my vows, a knock at the door heralded my mates Jazz and Miller arriving to celebrate the birth of my daughter. They had brought two cases of Red Stripe. Well, what was I to do? I had to wet the baby's head, didn't I?

We cracked open a few cans and turned on the TV. The night became a blur of drunken stupor and baby talk. The solemn promise I had made to my partner, my baby and myself had lasted all of a couple of hours.

***

Soon a chance presented itself to do what I had dreamed of doing: working full time as a DJ. During my time working at Sammy's, my interest in music had blossomed and I had hassled the resident DJ to teach me to use the decks. After a time he had given in and each night before the club opened he would let me play some tunes. I had loved it in the DJ box, and that passion was about to have a profound impact on the rest of my life.

It began on a Tuesday night when John, the regular DJ, failed to turn up for work. Dave, one of the managers at Crystals, knew that I understood the equipment and asked me to hop into the DJ box and play a few records. I could work the decks, and I jumped at the opportunity to escape from working behind the bar.

It ended up being a busy night and, luckily for me, one of John's record boxes was full of the rave tunes my friends and I listened to. There were only about twenty-five records in the box, so most of them got played twice, but the dance floor heaved all night.

Dave thanked me for stepping in and rewarded me by wiping out my bar tab for the night, which I might add was a considerable amount even by my standards! John failed to show up again the following Friday and I stepped in once more. Like the week before, the punters filled the dance floor all night. Some of the 'Sharon and Tracy' crowd moaned about the rave music, but most people, and especially the younger and trendier crowd, had a great time.

The following week, Dave informed me John wouldn't be returning and asked if I would like to DJ on a regular basis. I couldn't believe my ears! Being a DJ was a dream and I had just landed a job in the top club in town. I asked Dave for a budget to buy some records and he gave me an advance on my wages. I had to pay this back in weekly instalments.

I virtually sprinted to my mate Jason's record shop, the brilliantly named Left-Legged Pineapple. I spent every penny on the latest house tunes and the following Friday night was fantastic. By the end of it I had got through about ten pints of lager and a couple of bottles of wine. This was definitely my dream job.

Throwing myself into it one hundred percent and then some, I designed a promotional flyer to advertise Fridays at Crystals and named my night Desire.

I loved the Friday nights DJing, and although my hellish trip a few years before had put me off drugs I was now dabbling in amphetamines. Every person in the club was off their face on whizz or Es (ecstasy), but I would just have half a wrap of whizz to keep me buzzing and, if I'm honest, I took it because it enabled me to drink more.

Early doors, a young Italian lad called Pasquale started to turn up and hang around the DJ box. He reminded me of how I had been a couple of years earlier at Sammy's. Pasq loved house music and it seduced him just as it had me. I told him to start bringing a few records so he could play the warm-up slot before the club got busy.

As it turned out, he was a good DJ and had fantastic taste in music. We got on so well I eventually came to look on him like the younger brother I had never had. He wasn't a big lad and was more of a lover than a fighter. He never gave anyone any hassle, so the night trouble came his way I felt obliged to step in and fight his corner.

He had come up to me at the DJ box looking worried. I asked him what the problem was and he pointed out a group of lads who were giving him hassle, accusing him of trying it on with one of their birds. As I looked over at them, one of the group – a particularly skinny looking weasel of a lad – stood with his carpet-carrying arms, giving the impression that he thought himself to be tougher than he was. He caught me looking and took on a John Wayne stance. I told Pasq to stay near the DJ box and ignore them.

I turned away, put the next record on and took a drink. When I turned back the weasel and his mates had gathered around Pasq and were threatening him. 'The cheeky bastard,' I thought. I felt the familiar surge of adrenaline hit me and, without stopping to think, my headphones were off and I was out of the DJ box.

I moved straight in between Pasq and the lads and asked them what the problem was. The weasel got all animated and lifted his hands. As he did, I noticed he was holding a bottle. I moved swiftly. With my left hand I grabbed the bottle and with my right I power-slapped him (a technique my brother John had taught me). The weasel crumpled like a cheap suit and hit the deck.

One of the other lads ran off, but the third fancied his chances and drove forward. He met my short left hook straight to his jaw. He went reeling back, but the red mist had fallen and I went steaming forwards, punching him from as many different angles as possible. He didn't know what had fucking hit him. At that point the doormen came running upstairs and jumped in. When I told them what had gone on they took them straight out of the club.

When I returned to Pasq, I found him standing and staring in a state of shock. I handed him a bottle of Budweiser, got back in the DJ box and changed the record. As far as I was concerned that was the end of the matter.

A few weeks later the manager Dave told me the police had been looking for me. I went to the station to see what the problem was. It turned out the weasel had suffered a perforated eardrum and the thought of compensation had spurred him on to press charges against me. They arrested me, charged me with ABH (assault occasioning actual bodily harm) and summoned me to the Crown Court.

On the day of the hearing I was shitting myself as my solicitor had told me to expect a prison sentence. I couldn't believe the weasel and his mates had started a fight with Pasq, a lad who would never start a fight even if he could. No offence to him, but Pasq just wasn't the fighting type. Then when the weasel came out on the losing side, he ran off to the police. He was what I considered back then a grass and a guttersnipe.

The jury found me guilty. Apparently, sticking up for a friend who was just about to have a bottle rammed into his face wasn't enough to justify dropping the weasel and his mate. The judge sentenced me to a hundred and fifty hours of community service as well as ordering me to pay £750 in compensation and £250 in court costs. It seemed that crime really did pay for the weasel that day.

I continued working as a DJ and started pretending to Emma that it was more than the two nights a week so I could go out and drink with my mates without any hassle. As things went from strength to strength and we were attracting kids from all over the county, it wasn't long before I was a 'proper' DJ, working four nights each week (without pretending).

The frantic pace of all these changes in my life occupied me to a point that blinded me to whatever else was going on. All the DJ work and drinking meant that I neglected my duties as a father and as a partner to my very lonely girlfriend. But I had found the time to get Emma pregnant again and we had a second baby girl, Amber; another little beauty. Once more I promised to stop drinking and become a better father. But yet again, I failed miserably.

With two daughters, Emma and I had been able to move out of the council flat and into a council house. We started to decorate and I promised to get it looking nice for her and the kids. It all began well and the house started to become more of a home.

But the lads who owned Crystals at the time had been so successful that they had opened a bar called Busters directly opposite the club. It took no time for Busters to become the town's number one bar and my regular watering hole. And so the pattern of my life was set. I was either working and getting drunk or going out with my mates and getting drunk, seven nights a week.

Me and Mum 1970's

Home life 1980's

Working on my first scooter: wanting to be like my big brothers.

Skinhead 1983

Dedicated follower of fashion: 80's casual.

My Dad.

Twelve

Small Man Syndrome

Despite my pattern of drinking every night I still trained hard. I had first started physical training at the age of eleven. In my teenage years, Eamon and I ran the four miles to Mountsorrel Boxing Club, trained for a couple of hours and then ran back home. Or if we were lucky we got a lift in the back of a pickup truck owned by John's friend Ken.

One day when I got home from school I saw that my elder brothers had hung a punch bag in the back garden. I used to watch them working out with it and whenever they weren't around I copied what they did. I tried to emulate the moves of the great Muhammad Ali or my own favourite, Sugar Ray Leonard. I will always remember how boxing cemented me and my dad's time together as we sat up late to watch the great boxers of the 1980s battle it out in what, in my opinion, continues to be the greatest era professional boxing has ever seen.

I started to study Lau Gar Kung Fu under the tuition of Steve Faulkner. I loved the fact that you could use your feet to fight as well as your fists. I attended Steve's club every Sunday and soon started to climb the grades, although my Shelly Skins years saw me lapse and stop going altogether.

Once these skinhead years were behind me I returned to martial arts training under one of Steve's black belts, a guy called Ian. A small-framed man, Ian had a punch like a kicking donkey and was as fast as lightening. I was amazed at the way this guy moved when he sparred and I tried to imitate him in every way. I loved sparring and became good at it very quickly.

Eventually, my brothers opened their own kickboxing school and I continued to train alongside them for a number of years. We trained three times a week and the classes were very tough. Though populated with some of the hardest young lads from around town, it was not uncommon to see two or three people knocked unconscious in every two-hour session. These were some of the toughest sessions I have ever taken part in. Many were 'full contact' in every way.

My enthusiasm for training with these lads enabled me to qualify for a few competitions. I won Best Fighter of the Day at one event and gained first and second places on other occasions. My love of this sport extended further than enjoying the physical benefits, as I found it freed me from the thoughts of the abuse I had suffered, which always clouded my mind.

But the nonstop nights on the lash eventually took their toll and in the end I gave up on kickboxing while I was still a brown belt. Walking away from the sport I loved, the most positive thing in my life at the time, added to the demons that were constantly eating away at me. Having said that, my training had without doubt laid in me the foundations of what would ultimately prove to be my one of my saving graces.

As it does with most people, my drinking turned me into a horrible arsehole. I wasn't all that tough, but when I was drunk I always ended up fighting. I now know that I suffered from a classic case of 'Small Man Syndrome', which led me to believe that I always had to prove myself as a man. Whenever I was under the influence and bereft of common sense, that is what I would set out to do. Many times I ended up scrapping with someone for a trivial reason of my own creation, the worst of which being that they were looking at me or 'screwing me out'.

Somehow I always managed to convince myself when it all kicked off that the fights were never my fault. And though ashamed of them now, it wouldn't be a true autobiography without including some of the more vicious things I did. In doing so I am not elevating them in any way, just telling it how it was and how I saw it through my stupor.

One night while waiting for service at the bar in Busters with Adi, an off-duty soldier asked me what I was looking at. How dare he?

I told him straight: "You, you ugly cunt."

He moved forward and I gave him a roundhouse kick to the head, knocking him out cold. A decisive right cross to his mate's chin ensured that he would not be joining the action. I took my pint of lager off the bar and carried on chatting to Adi as if nothing had happened.

On another occasion, Adi and I stood at the bar during the annual street fair. A group of lads wearing comical, oversized hats started larking about. One of them kept bumping into Adi and laughing. Looking back, I don't think he had any malicious intent, but that wasn't how we saw it then.

Adi got pissed off and pulled the hat down over the lad's face. Then one of his mates threw a punch that just missed the side of Adi's head. I ran in with a front kick and dropped one of them. Adi grabbed a bar stool and started battering two of the others and I picked up a steel chair and slammed it into the mouth of another, knocking out a couple of teeth. By the time Adi had finished, a stump of one leg of the barstool was all he had left in his hand.

The doormen cleared the lads out and allowed us to stay. They knew us and we spent most of our time in Busters. We were accepted as members of this ugly scene.

This lifestyle and my heavy drinking contributed to me being a failure as a father and not much use as a partner to Emma. When she asked me to leave it gutted me, but I had nobody to blame but myself. Being continuously drunk had done nothing to prevent the breakdown of our relationship.

The brutality continued. It was me against the world, my world; a hazy, lonely world seen from a bar stool in Busters. I took on anyone that I thought was violating my own rules.

One such time was on a quiet Monday night. Two young DJs, Sam and Eddie, were doing their best to entertain a half-empty bar when a couple of local, heavily tattooed villains thought it would be funny to hassle them. It pissed me off as I sat watching these forty-year-old tough guys, who I knew had a reputation for violence, chipping away at an increasingly worried Sam and Eddie. They were pressuring them to play records they just didn't have.

After a while I stood up and politely asked them to stay out of the DJ box. They both moved forward to press-gang me, but I stepped backwards and to the side and raised my hands to chest height. I told them I didn't want to fight them and pushed my hands forward to create space between me and them. I then asked one of them, "Don't I know you?"

I knew exactly who he was: a mean bastard with a reputation. As he started to answer me, I launched a mighty right hook into his chin. The crack of his jaw breaking filled the room and he fell straight to the floor. I swung my left into his mate's face and he reeled back into the pinball machine. I front-kicked him to the nose and threw a left uppercut to put him away. Then my attention returned to his mate, who had rolled up in a ball and was screaming like a baby. I stamped on his head, shouting all the names I could think of.

By this time, Sam and Eddie had fled the DJ box and locked themselves in the upstairs office. I dragged both of these broken men out of the bar and shoved them in a heap on the pavement of the high street.

I closed and locked the front doors and walked upstairs to the office where Sam and Eddie stood, their bodies shaking with fear. I saw tears glistening in Sam's eyes. They said it wasn't the two guys who had scared them, but the explosion of violence I had released. With the benefit of hindsight, I know I should have thought about what they were saying. As it was, I returned to the bar and drank for free for the rest of the night.

Some of the violent encounters I was involved in at Busters blur into one another, there were so many of them. But the night I stood near the door with Rob and about ten of my mates and took 'The Brummie' out stays with me.

The pub was scarcely populated and over at the bar stood The Brummie. Known for his snideness, he was a sneaky fucker who wouldn't think twice about slipping a blade between your ribs. He had this desperation to be a known figure around the town. Having just moved from Birmingham he had put the rumour around that back where he lived he was 'The Man'.

A few people had fallen for his line, but I knew he was a fake and his claims held little weight with me. When a few weeks earlier he had offered me out and I had called his bluff, he had bottled it in front of everyone. This meant I had exposed him for the fraud he was and I knew he would want revenge.

As the evening progressed, I noticed him talking to one of my mates along the line. Behind his back he held a half-drunk bottle of wine. I knew what he was up to as he made his way towards me, chatting to this one and that. I knew that bottle had my name on it.

I adjusted myself so as not to alert him and saw at that moment that Rob was also aware of what was going on. As The Brummie came up to me, Rob went to say something, but before he could I launched a vicious, relentless attack on The Brummie, knocking him to the floor.

I kicked the wine bottle out of his hand and kicked him across the pub floor. The doormen came running in and asked me what was going on. I told them how The Brummie had tried to sniper me. They dragged him out by the neck and barred him. I returned to my mates and Rob confirmed that he was just about to tell me what was coming. He hadn't needed to as I was too alert and aware of my surroundings for an amateur like The Brummie to catch me out. I had dealt with it swiftly.

Over the years of working in the nightclub, pub and bar business and spending so much of my spare time out there among the punters, I have seen violence on levels that would make most decent people sick. I have seen stabbings, people with their faces ripped open by broken glasses and their heads stamped on. I have seen lives ruined and even lives lost. And I have learned one thing from it all: alcohol fuels outbreaks of pointless violence and I know, beyond doubt, that it really is the 'demon drink'.

Thirteen

Saturday Dad

I had found a home living with a group of lads in a shared house and was hanging around with Jay, one of the original Shelly Skins back in the day. He was known as 'Ryder' on account of the fact that he looked like Shaun Ryder from the Happy Mondays. Ryder has always been one of the best friends I have ever had.

Back then, he was another crazy drinker and he and I had some of the best, or should I say 'worst' sessions ever, as I was getting hopelessly drunk every night and kidding myself that life was good. Ryder and I would go all over the country on weekend drinking sprees, spending hundreds of pounds on booze, women and hotel rooms.

My DJ work had dried up. The lads who owned the club had sold up and opened another nightclub, The Emporium, in the nearby former mining town of Coalville. The Emporium fast became one of the UK's leading dance venues and achieved truly legendary status.

They employed other DJs to work as residents at their new dance nights and chose to leave me behind. To tell you the truth, it gutted me that they did this. It wasn't that I was jealous as such, but I had been with them from the very start and now they had left me on the shelf.

I sold my extensive record collection for a pittance and drank the money in one weekend with Ryder. We went to Sheffield. I love Sheffield. The people are friendly and I found it to be a place where I could be myself. It's also a city full of great-looking girls. Someone as ugly as Quasimodo could pull there, so I was confident that even Ryder might manage!

Although challenged in the 'looks' area, Ryder is known for packing a mighty punch in the trouser department and was always happy to display his impressive weaponry at the slightest opportunity. Well lubricated after consuming a bottle of wine and a few shorts in our hotel, we reached the first bar. While Ryder went to get the drinks I looked around for talent. I found it in two very good-looking girls sitting in a corner, so I sat myself as close to them as I could.

When Ryder came back from the bar with a couple of pints and a chaser each, I could tell by his face that he was pleased with my scouting. Taking a swig of his lager swiftly followed by a shot of his brandy, he took out his cigarettes, handed me one and then offered them to the girls. They declined, and in his silver-tongued way, said: "And fuck you very much, too."

The girls just sneered at him. Not one to miss an opportunity, Ryder winked at me and, unseen by the girls, unzipped his jeans and hung out his cock. He turned to one of the girls and politely apologised to her for his remark. She responded well and started chatting to him.

The humour of the situation had me bent over with laughter and I wasn't alone; the doormen and a few other lads in the bar had noticed and were laughing along. After about ten minutes of chat, Ryder pointed down to his lap, assuming she hadn't noticed. He smiled and said: "What you think to that, then?"

The girl just turned her nose up and, in an ever-so-polite way, said: "Yeah, I noticed it ages ago, but I've had bigger." The entire place erupted.

Ryder and I had many nights out full of fun and beer, and I enjoyed every one of them on the surface. How could I not? Time with a good and loyal mate is all anyone needs when they are down. And underneath all of the revelry, I was down. Deep inside of me, gnawing away, was a depression I couldn't shake.

On the Saturdays when I wasn't hungover or still drunk from the night before, I would pick my girls up and take them into town. This sounds good and it should have been, but even as a part-time Saturday dad I was useless. A few hours at the cinema or the local park was all I managed before the pub called to me and then, like me as a kid, they had to suffer the smell, the atmosphere and the sight of their dad getting drunk. The only difference was that they could do so from inside the walls that used to keep me out.

My drinking became so habitual that in the end I spent more time in the pub than anywhere else and became a dad of broken promises. Fuelled by whisky one Saturday night, and with the sweets I had bought for them still in my pocket, it seemed logical to me that as I hadn't kept my promise to pick the girls up earlier in the day I could visit them at home instead.

In answer to my knocking and calling out, Emma came to the upstairs window and refused to let me in. This was unusual, as no matter how badly I treated her she never once refused me when I wanted to see my children. Then again, this was at four o'clock in the morning.

Emma asked me to leave, but I became irate and started shouting even louder. I made it clear that I wasn't leaving until I had seen my girls as I was their dad. Looking back, I realise this was probably the overstatement of the year. I wasn't a father to my kids at all; I was a drunk who turned up when I felt like it and expected everything to be fine.

This time I stood outside Emma's house with a bottle of whisky in hand, demanding my rights. Emma called the police. They arrived and tried to politely persuade me to go home, but I had no home. I hadn't been paying my share of the rent and was homeless. My clothes were stored in a shed at a mate's place.

The police had tried to be nice, but they were losing patience. They told me that if I didn't move on they would arrest me. They didn't take kindly to my reply of, "Get fucked". Strong hands grabbed me and I felt the cold steel of the handcuffs they tried to shackle me with.

My instinct kicked in and, like a tiger wanting out of his cage, I charged at the police officer and pushed him to the floor. Something penetrated my sodden brain and told me I was now in deep shit. In this particular fight or flight situation, I ran. This was not a good choice, as my pissed up legs wouldn't even walk for me let alone run!

I awoke in a police cell with a banging headache and the hangover from hell. Without me knowing how or what had happened, I found myself stood in the dock facing the magistrate. Bile tried to rise from my stomach to my throat. It took all the willpower I had to stop myself chucking up.

The magistrate looked me up and down and pointed out the state I was in. A trail of vomit ran down the front of my shirt and dried blood caked my hands. Something like shame entered me as I realised, like the scum they must have thought I was, that the coppers had taken me to court without even thinking that I might have liked the opportunity to have a wash.

They barred me from visiting Emma's house, but for some reason, and very luckily, they didn't charge me for pushing the police officer. Even so, I left court that day feeling at the lowest point in my life so far.

Fourteen

My Own Dad

Diagnosed with mouth and tongue cancer caused by years of alcohol abuse and cigarette smoking, my dad's weight dropped to six stone and he was bedridden for months. Mum fed him and gave him bed baths in a daily toil that she never flinched from and carried out with her once more fixed smile and cheerful way.

Though weak in body, Dad found all of his old mental strength and willpower. He was determined not to let this cancer beat him and it didn't. He went into remission and became a new man. He still loved betting on the greyhounds, but he never drank or smoked again.

He went to church every Sunday and I finally got to see my dad as I remembered him from childhood. Through these later, sober years of his we would laugh together, watch films together and he would give me what he termed 'a latch-lifter'; the first few quid that got you into the bar.

One of my best moments and one that still fills me with joy is when I think about the time I caught a glimpse of Mum and Dad walking back from the fields hand in hand, smiling away. All the bitterness and bickering of my time at the bottom of the stairs in the cold hall had gone. I had truly found my dad again and Mum had her lovely Irish lad back.

A couple of years down the line I was working with Darren from Sammy's, helping him to tile a floor in a nightclub that was undergoing a refit. The telephone rang. It was Helen asking me to go to Mum and Dad's house straight away.

I turned to Darren and said, "My dad's dead." He asked me if that was what my sister had said.

I said that it wasn't, but I knew that was what had happened. He told me not to be so stupid, trying in his way to make things better, but the feeling of dread would not lift from me.

In the taxi on the way to the small, white bungalow they had moved into when all of us kids had flown the nest, it didn't seem real to me that everything around looked and carried on as normal while inside me a heavy, lead-laden feeling churned my stomach.

When I arrived, time seemed to slow down. The sun shone, giving everything a bright, lifted feel, but a slight breeze chilled my bones. As I walked over the grass towards the bungalow, Helen came out to meet me. Tears ran down my face. I knew without her telling me that Dad had passed away.

Helen cuddled me and held me tight, just like she used to when she looked after us all those years ago. She asked me to go in and see him. She said he looked happy, but I couldn't do it. I wanted to remember him as he was the last time I saw him and not as a lifeless corpse.

Looking towards Mum and Dad's gate, the memory came to me of how, on my last visit, Dad had given me some money to go out in town and had then stood at the gate waving me off. His jet black hair had looked pristine and he had worn a smart brown-and-white patterned cardigan with beige slacks over the top of his highly polished shoes.

I left Helen and went straight to Emma's house to tell her and my girls that Granddad had passed away. Emma held me and comforted me. Even though my uncontrollable drinking meant I had treated Emma like shit, she was still there for me at this terrible time.

My dad had known everyone in Loughborough and the respect they had for him showed at his funeral. More than two hundred people turned up to see him off. My brothers carried his coffin to the local church, followed by a procession of some of the most respected people in the town. I was proud to lead this procession.

We laid our dad, Samuel Skillen, to rest on October 13, 1998. He left us all a lasting memory of a loving father who got lost along the way but who never gave up on the journey and finally found his way home.

Fifteen

Wise Shakespearean Words

Somehow, amid the chaos of my life I met another lovely woman, Sarah. She cared for me and took me into her home. I still drank heavily, but like all alcoholics I had become good at hiding it. Sarah was a good soul and helped me get back on track.

I started to work as a DJ once more, this time in a local bar that quickly became one of the best venues in town. I played my beloved house music again and things were good. At this time, "good" meant that I was earning my own money again and getting free beer every night.

Even though I didn't start spinning my tunes until around half ten at night, I knew the owner, Gino, would stand me a few drinks before my shift, so I would turn up to work and start drinking at around eight. Gino, reputed to be a tight-fisted and temperamental old bugger, was nothing of the sort. He was always good to me and looked after me and I loved him for giving me another opportunity. I enjoyed working at Bar Europa and had some great times there.

Every Friday and Saturday night the bar filled to capacity and I played pumping house music until three in the morning. With the place rammed full, people took to dancing on the picnic-style tables Gino had put in the bar. This became a trademark and helped to create an electric atmosphere. In my opinion, Bar Europa during this period was the best bar Loughborough had ever had, made so by Gino's eccentric style of decoration and the free reign he gave the DJs who played there.

As far as my drinking habits went, there wasn't anything unusual in me downing an entire case of Budweiser and a bottle of wine while working and then heading off elsewhere once my shift ended. As had happened before, everything I did wore the label of me having fun, but swimming under the river of drink I consumed was the real me; a man suffering from bouts of depression every single day.

Sarah took this in her stride very well. Her family took me in and were the loveliest people I had ever met. For the first time since I was a small boy living in Manor Drive, I felt accepted and part of a family. Sarah worked for Carmel, a really nice woman who, brought up on the same street as me, was the daughter of my mum's best friend Cath. We got on really well together, as we did with Carmel's husband Ev.

As things progressed, Sarah and I virtually lived with Carmel and Ev until they bought a pub in a local village and Sarah took over the running of their other business. I moved with her into a large house in the village of Mountsorrel and at first everything went well.

Carmel had created a fantastic traditional pub atmosphere and the pub fast became the place to be in the village. It became our regular haunt and our drinking sessions went on late into the night. It was here that I met Paul, a massive-framed man with a huge beard.

Paul looked as mean as they come and everybody in the pub knew not to mess with him. It turned out he was the bouncer, Haystacks, from the roller disco I had attended in my youth. Paul was a kind-hearted soul, famed for the amount of Guinness he could drink.

One Bank Holiday Monday I tried to keep up with him. It was a huge mistake on my part. When I passed out around twelve hours later after fifteen pints of Guinness, Paul still stood at the bar as if he was on his first. I believe his personal record was around thirty pints!

Generally, Sarah and I had a happy time until, of course, I started to take the piss. When we drank I was always the first to start and the last to finish and, as always happened, I began to push Sarah away.

I have had some beautiful girlfriends in my past and have often wondered what on earth they saw in me. But the longer I seemed to be with them and the closer we seemed to get, the more my behaviour would push them away.

I would do my best to behave as badly as possible and when they had had enough and walked away, I would vindicate myself by putting all the blame on them and thinking that they never really cared for me. It was like some kind of self-deprivation. No matter how nice they were, I would find a way for it to end. Usually this came in the form of jealousy, which was a result of my own insecurities.

One time after a particularly bad argument with a previous girlfriend, Matt – a lovely lad from Huddersfield, who I love dearly – gave me a piece of paper. On it he had written: "Beware, my friend, of the green-eyed monster, because it doth mock the meat it feeds on."

He told me this was a line from Shakespeare's *Othello*. I kept this piece of paper with me at all times and tried my best to follow it, but it had come too late to save that relationship and once more I lost a girl I idolised but didn't know how to love.

Matt and his lovely wife Sharon are the subject of one of the most stupid things I have ever done and one of my biggest regrets. To this moment, I am highly embarrassed when I even think about it. No matter how much I try, I cannot apologise enough or forgive myself and here is why.

Matt had met Sharon while working with me at Pulse Nightclub. She is a stunning, red-headed beauty and Matt fell for her at first sight. I can't blame him, as not only is she a great-looking woman; she also has a fantastic sense of humour and loves Matt to bits.

I felt honoured to receive an invitation to their wedding, but as on any other occasion I arrived fuelled with too much drink. The ceremony in the church went well, but the reception presented even more opportunity to drink. I downed everything I could and became steaming drunk.

Once the formalities and speeches were over, the music started up. Matt and Sharon took to the floor to dance their first dance as man and wife. They looked beautiful and their parents and grandparents looked on with pride. But my drink-sodden brain didn't distinguish between this being a special moment for them, which didn't involve me, and other times when we had laughed at everything the way friends do. I saw only a chance to play a prank on them. It wasn't the time or the place, but I didn't have any sense or restrictions or boundaries. I had drowned any sense of propriety.

I swaggered over to the happy couple with a silly grin on my face, camera in hand, and to the horror of everyone present lifted the bride's dress and took a photograph!

The sudden silence of the guests was followed by gasps of "Oh no!" and "Oh God!" The acrid smell of burning material alerted me to the fact that something was amiss. As if the humiliation of the bride wasn't enough, the cigarette in my other hand had set Sharon's gorgeous dress alight.

A sudden moment of clarity hit me and I could have died on the spot. What the fuck was I doing? In front of a whole wedding reception on what was supposed to be the happiest day of my best friend's life, I had ruined their first dance as a married couple, insulted them both and, to cap it all, torched the bride!

I ran out of the room with my drunken head hung in shame. Sharon came after me and asked me to stay. She said she wasn't bothered and it was only a dress anyway. I couldn't believe how she could forgive me for such a stupid drunken act.

Even now, years later, the embarrassment comes flooding back every time I see Matt or Sharon. I wish I could turn back the clock and give them back their first dance together. Of all the terrible things I recall from my drinking days, this has to be one of the worst and I will always be truly sorry for it.

Sixteen

A Geographical Turning Point

My relationship with Sarah hung on a thread and I did nothing to strengthen it, even though she had tried everything to help me make my life work. She had arranged for me to see my children again and had taken us on some lovely days out. My girls loved her. But drink addiction is a selfish disease and its need takes over and destroys everything good.

Once again I started going out around town more and more, often ringing Sarah at four or five in the morning to come and pick me up. Understandably, her patience wore thin and she became fed up with me and my ways. Before long she told me it was over.

I moved into a one-bedroom flat and began drinking alone, a sure sign of a desperate man. Hitting the town earlier and earlier, my life deteriorated into a constant cycle of hangovers and long drinking sessions.

Although I was never a street drinker, I did mix with other hardcore drinkers in the lowliest of bars. We were all fellow outcasts on the very edge of society, all looking for answers and making the same mistake of looking in the wrong places.

I wasn't going to find a life worth living among these thieves, fighters, gamblers and one-time somebodies who propped up the bars of the worst drinking holes I now attended on a daily and nightly basis. The people I mixed with had already given up on life and I had fallen into their fold. I wasn't working and my existence became a beggar's search for the next hit of alcohol.

I didn't really care who bought it for me, but I needed it and this need consumed me. My only thought, even when stood in front of a full glass, was where the next drink would come from. I had become so preoccupied with getting my next drink that I never enjoyed the one I already had.

Most of my days I scrounged around the arcade looking for tokens or free plays so I could win enough money to get my daily fix. Many a time on my way home to my desolate flat in a nearby village I would be so drunk that I would have to sit for a few hours to sober up before I could continue my walk.

One night, during my three-mile trek home at around four in the morning in the middle of an icy winter, I stopped to piss behind a bush by the side of the road along the bypass. I couldn't get my zip undone and ended up pissing myself and falling into a ditch.

I was so drunk that two hours passed before I woke up, and by that time my trousers had frozen almost solid. My bones hurt with the cold as I crawled out of the ditch. I made my way back to my empty, soulless bedsit and ran a bath, forgetting that I hadn't any electricity or gas until I felt the water and found that it was as cold as I was. I had spent my benefit cheque on the previous night out.

I had to find a way of warming up. I felt ill and thought I was going to die. I turned to leave the bathroom and caught a glimpse of myself in the mirror. Blood and vomit stained my shirt and my hair was matted to my head with dirt.

My hangover started to kick in and I felt sicker than ever. My stomach turned and my body ached with cold. I was starving hungry, but even if I had had any food to eat I knew my stomach would have rejected it. I went to the kitchen to get myself a hot drink, but there was no milk or sugar, just a single teabag. I put it in the cup and, forgetting I had no way of heating it, went to switch on the kettle. My heart sank when I remembered. I threw the cup down and slid to the floor. I was destitute and knew things had to change. I had to do something.

I sat there on the cold, red-tiled floor and wept, my teeth chattering in the freezing cold. I eventually got up and made my way into the front room, where my bed was. My thin, bony body slumped across my old mattress underneath a quilt that hadn't seen the inside of a washing machine for weeks. I rubbed my cold skin and feet up and down, wishing I had a few old coats for extra warmth.

Eventually I passed out. I awoke later that day, warm but hungry and full of self-pity. Once again I knew it had to stop. Fear clutched my chest as the events of the previous night came back to me. How had I survived out there in that ditch on such a cold night?

Then I realised that the obsessive nature of my drinking had finally brought me to my knees. I looked around my lonely, empty excuse for a home. I had wanted to decorate when I first moved in, but as soon as I got my first bit of money I had spent it on a massive drinking spree instead. I had lost everything that was ever any good in my life and instead of being in the company of family and friends I lived my life in the lowly bars of the walking dead.

I had become a lonely, drunken wreck. Coming to this realisation hurt, but it reinforced my resolve that I had to do something; I had to change something. I dressed and went into town, determined to try to sort my life out. I only knew one place where I could sit and plan my future. The pub.

Eddie, the DJ from Busters, gave me what seemed like a solution. He and some of the local lads were planning on going to Greece to work the summer season. They had been there every year for the past few and had always had a great time. I thought this sounded like an excellent idea and that maybe if I could get away from Loughborough I could turn things around.

I needed funds to get started, so I went to see Sarah. I'm not sure if it was out of the goodness of her heart or in desperation to get me out of her hair, but she agreed to help me and within a couple of weeks I flew off to my new beginning.

Sadness hit me as soon as I landed in Faliraki. It was a deep, depressing sadness I had never known before. I tried to console myself with drink, but to no avail. On that first night lying in a rundown apartment with mosquitoes eating me alive, I realised I had made one big mistake. How the fuck was I, a man who spent ninety-nine percent of his time in the pub, ever going to get better by going to one of the drinking capitals of Europe?!

Over the following few days I fell into previous patterns of my life: drinking and DJing. The bar owner liked me and offered me a job for the season if I wanted it, but I couldn't shake this terrible sadness. I missed my girls and the depression swamped me.

One morning I woke up, went straight to the nearest shop and bought a bottle of vodka. Then I headed to the beach. The beauty surrounding me – white sand and blue sea lapping the shore in never-ending gentle waves – did nothing to lift me. I wanted only the solace the fiery liquid could give me. A few drinks in and my hazy gaze into nothingness gave me no self-awareness; just a deep need for my anguish to end.

I don't know what stopped me from walking into the water, because the thought of my body swirling around and then being tossed into the depths of emptiness appealed more than the reality I knew I had to face. As I dwelt more on what I longed for, it came to me that I didn't want to suffer any more and that's what had been happening to me. For years I had been suffering, lost in a meaningless life like a wandering vagabond, drifting from one day to the next.

Since the earliest years of my life I had known hardship, but I had always searched in the wrong places for a way out. My world existed beyond reality. I hadn't solved any of my problems or grown above them. I had tried to drown them or block them out. During the process I had rejected anything good that came my way and given prominence in my life to anything that gave me temporary respite from the stuff I couldn't deal with.

There is no hardship I had ever been through that matched this self-analysis; this realisation that, in the end, it had all been down to me. The hurt cut into me and the wounds of it bled invisible, painful blood that sweated from every pore of my body and rained torrents of tears down my face. My world darkened. I needed to end it all, to leave it all behind.

A peace came over me, and with my decision made I just needed to think through how to end my life. I began to go over the various ways in my mind, but two little girls kept dancing into my head and interrupting me. Their smiling, loving faces shattered the calm inside me and I knew at that lowest point that I had to try. I had to change.

I had to get my shit together and create a whole new life.

The bottle hurtled through the air, the remaining vodka glistening in the sun as it sprayed out. The splash it made when it landed in the sea sealed my determination. Had I really just discarded what had become my nectar? My hope lifted. I had taken my first step.

In the past I would have drunk every last drop before I teetered towards change, which is probably why it never happened. I took heart. If I had enough strength to reject just a little of what I had used as a lifeline and the answer to everything, I could find enough to turn from it forever.

Thanks to Helen's help in paying for my fare, I arrived home only five days after I had left and went straight to Sarah's house. She wasn't there, so I sat in her back garden and waited. The air chilled my wasted body. My mind sank into the depths of depression. Still soaked in vodka, I felt sick. Tiredness sapped me as the hours went by.

When Sarah eventually came home she was distraught at my return. She had suffered enough because of me and hadn't wanted me to come back. I persuaded her to let me stay the night. Standing under the shower with the hot water beating down on me eased some of the torment of our reunion until a strange feeling seeped over me.

Nauseous and dizzy, I sat on the bathroom floor to steady myself. As the waves of sickness erupted I crawled to the toilet and puked my guts up. A fear trickled through the horror of it. I thought I had gone too far. My destiny was no longer in my own hands. I would die there, slumped in a heap; a ball of nothing. I don't know how I got to bed, but when I fell asleep I sank into the most surreal dream of my life.

I stood on a conveyor belt looking down into a pit of fire. In the middle of the fire people were having sex, drinking and fighting. Terror gripped me. I felt I was looking upon my infinite future. I could almost feel the heat of the flames as my body swayed towards them, but a hand dug into my shoulder and held me back. I tried to turn around, but the hand prevented me.

The scene changed and I saw a mass riot in the streets of a burned-out city. Headless people ran around and hollow screams filled the air. I slipped and nearly fell, but the hand on my shoulder grabbed me. It was then that I heard a whisper in my ear. "Not yet," the voice said, "not yet."

This time the vision gave me a large, golden field. In the distance, a huge oak tree threw a soft, hazy shadow. Under the tree stood a well-dressed man playing golf. The warm sun shone in the sky and a gentle wind touched my face.

For the first time in years, the turmoil of sadness that had always been with me settled into a true calmness and I felt the real feeling of deep and complete happiness. My eyes squinted against the brilliant light as I tried to make out the man in the distance. He turned around and smiled. His beautiful complexion shone like gold in the sunlight and his smile lit up the sky with a rainbow of colours. It was my dad.

He looked so wonderfully happy and his strong, chiselled look had returned. He waved at me, smiled and the words from his mouth floated to me on the breeze. "Not yet," he said, "not yet."

Suddenly, the sky darkened and the beauty of the dream disappeared. Two massive, claw-like hands grabbed me round the waist and pulled me violently to the floor. I looked around. Gravestones were bursting out of the ground. I screamed; the rasping non-scream that never leaves the throat of those struck with terror while they sleep. The force pulled me further into the dirt and in my ear I could hear a brutal growling. I couldn't breathe. I was suffocating.

Panic catapulted my body awake and out of bed, but not out of the terrible nightmare that still clothed me in dread. My own cries assaulted my ears. My whole body cried tears: through my eyes, through my mind and through every pore of my body.

Sarah sat up as my fear had transmitted to her. But as the realisation of what was happening hit her, she reacted like she never had never before. Usually she would comfort me when my nightmares came, but this time I could feel her disgust as she left me and went to the bathroom. I sank to the floor, my naked body trembling. I held my head in my hands.

When Sarah returned I curled into a ball and pleaded with her to help me. She told me I had to sort myself out. I looked up into the mirror and saw the real me for the first time; a ravaged, eight-stone, desperate excuse for a human being on the edge of death.

To break the image I ran to the bathroom, turned on the taps and rinsed my face with cold water again and again. As I did so my real needs entered me. I didn't want to die, I wanted to live! I wanted my children, I wanted my dad back and I wanted my mum.

At some point during the torment that wracked me I drained

myself enough to fall into a deep sleep. When I woke I had the sense of having been cleansed and made ready for something new. Sarah gave me then what I most needed in the world: the support of someone who hadn't really given up on me.

She spoke to me about rehab. In my desperation I realised that this was my only hope of a new life, but I couldn't do it alone. Sarah was fantastic and contacted a rehab centre for me. They agreed to talk to me and to see if they could help. The day came when I was to visit a place called Gloucester House.

The drive to Gloucester House took us through some beautiful English countryside, but it all whizzed passed me without gaining my appreciation. Sarah drove and I sat stiff and fearful, part of me wanting to tell her to turn around at every junction, part of me holding out so much hope. I don't think any other Tuesday in my life has meant as much to me as that one did.

We came into the village of Highworth near Swindon and found the house nestled between a pub and an off-licence! The irony of this left me unsure whether to laugh or cry. But the one thing it told me was that the folk running this show must have some powerful tricks up their sleeves to help people cope with a consuming addiction when they can see and smell their weakness every day.

My legs shook as we approached the ornate entrance, which was covered by a sandstone archway. I pressed the button on the intercom and waited. The disengaged female voice that came crackling through the dozen tiny holes on the wall had a happy, welcoming sound to it, but even so I felt like saying, "Sorry, I have the wrong address". Instead, I gave my name. Her greeting coincided with the buzz of the lock being released. Sweat broke out on my forehead and my mouth dried out.

As I stepped inside, nothing about the place matched the preconceived ideas I had had. Instead of a hospital environment with porters and people in white coats bustling about, I walked into a churchlike, serene atmosphere, evoking the memory of the only other time I had felt anything like it; that happy moment in my dream.

The welcome continued as Sue, a lady I liked at once, and Dave, a hippy type of guy in a suit and glasses, greeted us. They showed Sarah into another room and led me into a communal room with wooden chairs around the walls and an old sofa set against one wall. A TV and video recorder stood in one corner and a selection of neatly stacked games and jigsaws stood on a shelf in another.

We all sat down. I was on one side and they were facing me. Sue had a notepad. Dave scrutinised me silently for a moment and then, instead of the question I expected ("Why do you think you should have a place here?"), he simply asked, "So, how are you?"

Nothing I had rehearsed prepared me for this and I didn't know how to answer. Dave gradually put me at ease, so much so that when I did start to talk I spilled out my entire life story in about the space of half an hour.

During this time I crossed a vital hurdle. I admitted for the first time ever to anyone other than myself that I had a bad drink problem. Dave's exclamation of, "No shit, Sherlock!" told me that he didn't think it would require the help of Dr Watson to suss that out. This was my kind of humour and it relaxed me even more. I began to feel more ready for the journey ahead than I had ever thought I would be.

After our chat they took me on a tour of the house. This converted, four-storey property with its high ceilings and decorative cornices still clung on to some of its former glory. However, these sadly came to an abrupt end wherever modern-day partition walls had cut through.

The first room leading off the hall held a pool table, and a little further along we came to a communal dining room that had the look and feel of a 1970s-style café with the biggest tea urn I had ever seen in one corner. I didn't know it then, but that tea urn and I were to become great friends!

The kitchen opened on to a small garden patio area. Two lads sat out there smoking rollups and drinking tea. They both greeted me with a friendly hello. One had a strong Liverpudlian accent and the other said something I couldn't quite make out due to his deep northern tones. I nodded and followed Dave and Sue into an office.

This room contained three desks and a mountain of books and other literature. An elderly lady sat at one of the desks and, like everyone I had met, she gave me a bright and cheerful hello. At that point, a middle-aged guy wearing work clothes came in and Dave introduced him as Roger. Roger, who ran the workshop, offered to show me around. He led me through to a room that was attached to the office.

A few people stood or sat at benches, one painting on glass and another using a lathe to turn wood. Once more I felt welcome as all of them looked up to say hello. At the other end of the workshop a door led into a small garden, where Sue joined us. They walked with me up to what they called the Green Room; an annexe situated next to a small bungalow that housed the women's quarters. When I became a resident I found that the

Green Room was where it all happened.

I spent about an hour or two talking to Sue and a few members of staff before I had to leave. As I thanked everyone, I knew I wanted so much to come and stay there. I wanted to tap into the hope they offered and as we left it felt like I was leaving a lifeline behind.

But I did have something to hang on to. They had told me that a place was mine if I wanted it. I have never wanted anything more! The problem was they couldn't say when. It could be several weeks or maybe even months before they had a vacancy.

I had been off the beer for a few days, as you couldn't visit Gloucester House unless you had been sober for at least three days. But I didn't know how long that would last without support. The very next day, a Wednesday, they called me. Someone had broken the strictest rule: residents must abstain from drink. The offender had to leave immediately and a place was now available. Could I get there on Friday, just two days later? I was in shock, but I agreed there and then.

Seventeen

A Chance to Turn My Life Around

I arrived at Gloucester House on a sunny afternoon in June 2001, scared shitless of what lay ahead but knowing that I had to go through with it. This time when I rang the buzzer the door opened, taking me into a whole new life.

The Liverpudlian lad who I had seen on the patio met me, shook my hand and, as he took my suitcase, said, "I'm Brian". I followed Brian through the house to a much smaller office I hadn't been in before.

The small, smartly dressed and very well-spoken man called David (not Dave the ex-hippy councillor, but David, the manager of Gloucester House) introduced himself to me. Books seemed to fill every bit of space in this office, and the most prominent was a Bible.

Many years had passed since I promised the truck driver who picked us up after our night in the cells that I would one day visit the Salvation Army, but I inadvertently found myself keeping it as Gloucester House is connected to the Salvation Army.

David sat me down and asked how I was feeling. I told him I was nervous and he said that was normal. To be honest, I had no recollection of what 'normal' was, so to me it wasn't normal at all.

David ran through the rules of the house and told me my 'buddy' for the first two weeks would be Brian. For the first week I must not leave the house and after that, for a further week, I must not do so unless accompanied by Brian. Lights

141

out was at 10.30pm and breakfast was at 7.30am. Smoking was only allowed in the dining room or outside and I could drink as much tea as I wanted.

After the formalities of signing the necessary forms, David called Brian in and asked him to show me to my room. We went up two flights of stairs and into a room at the front of the house. I looked through the window to a welcome view: the village square. This was the hub of Highworth, an old English village protected by a conservation order and home to one of the oldest churches in the country.

I sat on the bed and Brian left me to sort out my things. This welcome respite gave me the space to adjust to my new surroundings. The scent of freshly washed sheets in the warm evening air reminded me of my childhood when Mum would tuck me into bed. This evoked feelings that I needed time to deal with.

The room was the size of a decent double bedroom with a sink at the end of the single bed. That night, after putting my few clothes into the walnut wardrobe that stood next to my bed, I lay there thinking about how my life had panned out and what had brought me to a rehab centre that was more than a hundred miles away from home.

Then I noticed a Bible on the small cabinet next to my bed. I picked it up, opened a page and read the following words: "Yet what is a man profited if he gains the whole world and loses his own soul?"

These words hit me like a sledgehammer to the head and created a pivotal moment in my life. I felt the whole weight of the world lift from my back. Calmness entered me and I knew this was the place I was meant to be.

Later, when the lights went out, nervousness at what the future held filled my stomach with butterflies and kept me awake for most of the night. But as I lay gazing up at the stars through the open blind of my window, my nerves settled and turned into a mixture of anticipation and excitement. Eventually I drifted off to sleep.

The sun woke me the next morning, its warming rays falling across my face. Although I hadn't slept for many hours I felt as fresh as a daisy and had a sense of complete ease in my mind. For a moment I had forgotten where I was. Then the reality of my situation kicked in and so did the adrenalin.

I sat up in bed to gather my thoughts, but before I could discern how I felt about this new beginning to my life Brian knocked on my door, popped his head around, asked if I was OK and reminded me that I only had until 8.00am to get to breakfast. It was already 7.30.

There is nothing quite like the smell of an English breakfast, and it was this and the general chatter and clinking of knives and forks that welcomed me into the 'greasy spoon' atmosphere of the dining room.

There were a couple of lads and two women in the dining room and, as before, they all extended a friendly greeting to me. The lad I had seen on the patio with Brian on my first visit, 'Bradford John' as I came to call him, gestured to me to come and sit opposite him. On finding out that I didn't have any fags, he pushed a packet of tobacco and some papers towards me. I rolled myself a cigarette and lit up, grateful to have something to concentrate on.

As I relaxed and enjoyed the taste of the smoke and the steaming hot cup of tea Brian fetched for me, people began to file into the room, greeting each other and filling their plates with bacon, eggs, sausages and beans from the hot trays next to the tea urn.

Even though this was only the second time I had seen my ten or so fellow inmates and had never really met them, I had a strange sensation of knowing them. They were all in various stages of recovery, but they still had that look of certainty that was so familiar to me. I finished my cigarette and went to fetch some breakfast.

I hadn't eaten properly for years, and for the previous four years breakfast had been off the menu because I was usually just crawling into bed first thing in the morning. I made a brave attempt by putting a few items on my plate, but when I started to eat I felt like heaving, so I gave it a miss. After another cigarette, more tea and a Q&A session with my new friends, everyone took to his or her daily task of cleaning the house.

I learned that we all had a specific job on a weekly rota basis. My first job was to clean the brasses. Brian took me to the cleaning cupboard, gave me a tin of Brasso and a cloth and took the hoover out for himself. I had to polish the brass doorplates and handles and then move on to polishing the wooden furniture around the house.

I made my way to the bottom of the twisting stairwell and sprayed the banister rail. The smell of the polish filled my nostrils, transporting me once again to my childhood, to mornings spent with my mum cleaning Mrs Ashmore's house.

I missed Mum terribly, and at that moment I felt like a little boy living in the body of thirty-year-old man. My eyes filled with tears as I realised this was exactly what I was.

Mum had moved to Spain after the death of my father. I couldn't blame her, as I imagine living opposite the cemetery that housed the grave of the man she loved so dearly and spent forty years of her life with through thick and thin can't have been the happiest sight for her to wake up to each morning.

She had always held a deep longing inside her to travel. She often used to ask Dad to go abroad on holiday with her and his answer was always the same: "If I was meant to fly I would have been born with wings". Dad had many sayings that I never understood as a kid, but that I now see that many of them held great wisdom. "You'll have plenty of time to go abroad when I'm gone," he would say. Being the more romantic of the two, Mum seemed disappointed at this.

After my dad passed away I regularly went to stay with my mum. Her heart was broken and she had begun to hit the wine bottle behind closed doors. She tried to put on a brave face, but I knew that her world had crumbled. Stuck in that bungalow on an estate that housed people who were much older than her and with only memories of Dad to keep her company, she was never going to get any better.

We spoke about how she felt lost and alone. People had stopped coming to visit and she felt like a spare part with no future other than waiting to die. She was always so young at heart and to see her like this crushed me. I suggested that she went on holiday to Spain to stay with my brother Sam, who was living and working out there at the time. I reminded her that it was something she had always wanted to do and that Dad had always said she should when he had gone.

She arranged her holiday and flew off a couple of weeks later, and while she was away I stayed at her bungalow. She came back after a week, smiling and saying she had had a fantastic time but wished that Dad could have been with her. I could see in her eyes how exciting she had found it all. It was then that she said she could imagine living out there, and I said, "Why not?"

The next day she told me she had made the decision to sell up and go to live in Spain, where she stayed for nearly fifteen years.

Remembering this and longing to be with her brought me to the point of breaking down, but, like a timely saviour, the sound of Brian dropping the hoover down the stairs brought me back to reality. Instead of me bursting into tears, we both burst into fits of laughter as Brian followed the hoover.

Bradford John ran into the hallway to see what all the commotion was about, only to find Brian tangled in the hoover wire at the bottom of the stairs and both of us in hysterics. John smiled and helped me get Brian back on his feet again. The ice was broken and for the next six months the three of us shared tears of laughter and emotion in equal measure on a daily basis.

By nine o'clock, our morning chores were done. With my newly acquired knowledge that everyone had their own cup and drank copious amounts of tea and smoked rollups by the dozen, we headed off to the Green Room.

My first therapy session loomed and I had no idea what to expect. Dave and Sue arrived and we entered the plain and simple room with its calming green walls. Twenty or so chairs were placed around the edge and my nerves started to tingle in my stomach once more. We arranged our seats in a semicircle around Dave and Sue, who sat next to a white board at one end of the room.

Dave handed out the preamble, The Twelve Steps of Alcoholics Anonymous (AA) and my own copy of *The Big Book* (also from AA), which he told me to hang on to.

As I looked around the room at the group I realised that all of us brought something similar to the table. I could read it in the look of deep sadness in their eyes. Each had the look of somebody who is lost.

The preamble was read out, then chapter five of *The Big Book* and finally The Twelve Steps of AA. These short readings set the tone and laid out the rules of the session. Only truth and honesty were allowed in this room, and one or all of the group members would soon pull up anyone who tried to falsify their own story or lie in anyway way, shape or form.

When you become an alcoholic or addict you also become a good liar, and in those terms I was the heavyweight champion. You get so good at it you even start to believe your own lies. But there is a catch. You tell so many lies and spin so many stories that your own web of deceit entangles you and eventually you are the only one who believes it all. You tell tales that are so farfetched that 'normal' people think you have gone mad.

'P', an older, Irish lady, stood up and told her story. She had worked in Ireland at the height of the Troubles and had seen a lot of terrible things, as she put it. Her reason for getting lost in the bottle was the death of her young son.

Another lady stood up and spoke of how the husband she loved had used her as a punch bag. When it was Bradford John's turn he wouldn't talk, saying he wasn't ready. Brian told stories of his family and how the death of the mum he loved dearly turned him to the booze.

The stories kept coming. Each person started with a statement of what they were: an alcoholic or an addict. I began to question whether I had done the right thing by admitting myself to Gloucester House.

'S' stood up next and told his story. He was in the army and had been bullied, so he went AWOL. While on the run in Thailand he began working for people who turned out to be gangsters and they set him to work on a fishing vessel on the Indian Ocean. He told us how they treated him like a slave, threatening him with guns on a daily basis. Eventually he made his escape and returned to England.

After this, the room descended into deathly silence. Dave turned to me and asked if I would like to speak. I stood up and looked around the room. My stomach churned and beads of sweat broke out all over my body. And then I said the words that were to change my life forever: "Hi, my name is Peter Skillen and I am an alcoholic."

Smiles broke out around the room and the atmosphere lifted as everyone simultaneously said, "Hello, Peter". I stood for a moment and then told the room how I felt; that compared to them my story wasn't so bad, and how I was even starting to think that maybe I was OK. Everyone had a knowing look of amusement on their faces at this, and Dave asked, "Who here has said that before?"

They all raised their hands. Dave turned to me and said: "Everyone has their own hell, man." I sat back down and started to tell my story.

I talked about my childhood and the good times I had had as a very young child: the long, hot summers; the trolley races around Manor Drive; football with the local lads at the park; our treks to the top of Beacon Hill; building snowmen with my brothers; and cuddles from Mum and Dad. I was trying hard to avoid the hard times, but eventually I started to talk about those, too.

Not one person spoke, they just sat and listened. Nobody formed an opinion and everyone could empathise. For the first time in my life I felt like someone was listening to me. I told the room about how I hated my father's drinking and how jealous I was of my older brothers and sisters. They had had a hardworking father who loved and cared for them. As the youngest, I had been left with a drunken shadow of that man who scared me half to death on a nightly basis by threatening us all or convincing me that I was going to die with his rants about nuclear war. I spoke of the time another boy had ripped my innocence from me in a dirty allotment.

The tears started to flow and I sobbed as I told how we lived with no food or electricity for months on end because my dad had spent the money on alcohol. I told them about the violence and the drink and drugs that surrounded me and how, by the age of fourteen, I had been tattooed, smoked weed, drunk beer, fought for the pleasure of my brother and his friends, sniffed glue and petrol, snorted amphetamines off a toilet seat, been arrested and been left alone at night to fend for myself.

I finally broke down and told them how all I had ever wanted was to be a normal boy. I wanted to be in the school play or play football for the school team. I wanted to go to a school where they never called me by my last name or gave me an inferior stab at education because of that name.

I wanted to walk around a town where people didn't point their fingers and the local paper didn't carry my family's name every other week. I told them how I missed my children and how inadequate I was as a father. I told them how I regretted letting my children down and how disgusted I was at myself for losing every opportunity that I had ever had. I told them I didn't want to be an alcoholic or to go to bed every night wishing I wouldn't wake up. I told them all I wanted was a 'normal' life.

After I had spoken for about an hour, Dave asked everyone if they thought I was in the right place. The replies were unequivocal. One by one, people told me how my story confirmed that Gloucester House was exactly the place I should be. Dave added to these comments, telling me that if he didn't have the proof of his own eyes with me sat in front of him, but had heard my story from someone else, he wouldn't believe that I was still alive. He then said he thought this a good time to have a break.

We all filed outside for a smoke and each and every person that was in that room came and hugged me and reaffirmed for me that I was in the right place. My whole being felt at ease and I thought, 'Maybe now I really do have a chance to turn my life around'.

Eighteen

A Lesson Learned

I settled into the routine well, attending daily therapy sessions and making a chessboard and bird tables in the workshop to sell in the local community. In the evenings I enjoyed my leisure time with John and Brian playing pool or watching videos. Copious amounts of tea kept away our thirst and we smoked like chimneys, but we were sober.

Time passed and before I knew it I had gone a whole month without a drink and I felt good. I ate three or four meals a day and was in bed and asleep by half ten every night.

On warm evenings, the three of us sat on the steps at the front of Gloucester House talking for hours about our past experiences. Even Bradford John began to open up, finding the relaxed atmosphere drinking tea and smoking fags with his mates a safer place for him to do so than in the Green Room.

It was on one of these evenings that we encountered 'The Bullfrog', so called because of his tough, well-built, mouthy appearance. He and his cronies had been giving the people at the rehab centre a lot of hassle. They apparently thought it was funny to shout obscenities and ridicule them every time they met in the street. This particular night The Bullfrog thought it was a good idea to start on us and shouted something over.

As John got up to go inside, I remembered the days when I had bullied people just like this jerk was doing and how I had learned a lesson never to be forgotten. I told John not to worry about him as he was just a bully and the more he allowed himself to be intimidated, the more the lad would do it. The

Bullfrog shouted over again, calling us tramps and alkies. I stood up and screwed him out, purposely trying to catch his eye. Eventually I did. He looked over and asked who I was looking at, so I told him straight: "You, you cunt. Why?"

My answer took him by surprise as he wasn't used to anyone answering back. I stood there and continued to stare at him with eyes like laser beams as though I was drilling a huge hole right through his fucking head. He was ruining the peace and quiet I had experienced away from the brutal world I had lived in previously. And by doing so, this bully had evoked in me a reaction of wanting to tear him to pieces. This went against all I had spoken of since arriving at Gloucester House: my hatred of violence.

At that moment, one of the staff – a beautiful lady we all called Julie Andrews due to her softly-spoken voice and sweet manner – called to us to come inside as it was time for bed. On hearing this, The Bullfrog went into overdrive, laughing and shouting: "Run along girls, it's past your bedtime."

Yes, he could shout then, but one minute before the shot of adrenalin that had surged through his body when I called him a cunt had glued his boots to the floor. Then when he thought there was no threat, he bloated his big bullfrog chest and became louder than ever.

Though I was fired up, I did the right thing and went into the house with the others without saying anything more. We made our way to Brian's room at the top of the house for a last fag and a cup of tea together before turning in. Like mine, this room looked out over the square and we could hear The Bullfrog still shouting and performing for his bunch of weasel cronies down below.

The Bullfrog spotted me as I stood on Brian's bed and looked out of the window. His mouth slotted into gear, shouting at me and telling me I was lucky I had been sent to bed just in time. He added that the next time he saw me he was going to batter me to within an inch of my life. This enraged me. Here we were in rehab trying to get better and this fat cunt and his mates were trying to intimidate us. I had had enough.

"Oi, fat boy," I shouted down. He looked up and the square went quiet. "Meet me tomorrow at one o'clock on the football pitch at the top of the road and we can sort it out then."

The weasels all looked at their leader, waiting for his reply. "OK," he said, "I'll be there."

"Well then," I shouted back, "now we have that sorted, would you mind shutting the fuck up so we can get some fucking sleep?" With this I threw him a massive smile.

The weasels laughed, but The Bullfrog had no answer. I closed the window, sat down on the bed next to John, lit my rollup and sipped my tea. John asked if I really meant what I had said. I told him I did.

Bradford John started telling us how the lad had a reputation for being the toughest bloke in the village. I pointed out to him that I wasn't from the village, so I would be OK. This lightened the mood.

The next morning was Saturday and after doing our chores and having breakfast I went and bought some fruit and cheap tobacco from the small market in the square outside. The sun beamed down, filling me with a feel-good feeling. Back in my room I prepared myself for the one o'clock showdown. I put on my jeans, tied my work boots extra tight and slipped on the old t-shirt I wore for workshop sessions. On my way downstairs I bumped into Brian and John.

Brian asked me if I intended to carry out my offer of the night before. When I said I did he asked me not to, reminding me how much bigger The Bullfrog was than me and how he would probably turn up with his mates and batter me.

This didn't deter me. I knew the only way to stop the insults and the intimidation was to cut The Bullfrog down to size. I made my way up towards the football pitch and Brian followed, while John stayed at the house. I loved John, but although he came out with fantastical stories of fighting ten men at a time, Brian and I knew he was just a dreamer and that on the inside he was just like us all; a child trying to sort his life out and learning how to grow up.

The football pitch loomed like a Roman arena, ready to accept me against a pack of lions. Only there was no crowd jeering and no opponent ready to tear my heart out. We waited. My nerves jangled and Brian admitted that his shit was churning in his stomach. "You and me both," I told him.

The church clock struck once, like the bell of doom. Brian's voice shook with forced laughter. "Oh well, they can only kill us!" he said.

We stood and waited until 1.30pm, but nobody came. I looked at Brian and shrugged my shoulders. "His mates probably couldn't make it!"

Brian smiled and we walked back to Gloucester House. At around teatime, we sat out at the front of the house drinking tea, having a fag and listening to Bradford John telling us how lucky The Bullfrog had been in not turning up as he had followed us up to the pitch and had stood out of sight, just in case we needed his back up.

We knew he hadn't left the house, but we let him have his fantasies and didn't interrupt or call his bluff as he proceeded to tell us how next time he saw The Bullfrog he would batter him. As he started to shadowbox badly, showing us exactly what The Bullfrog would get, his intended quarry came around the corner. I couldn't help telling him, "Well now's your chance, because here he is..."

John wilted and his body slumped down beside me. "Fuck, he heard me. Don't let him hit me, Peter."

I stood up, shielding the frightened John, and stared at The Bullfrog as he walked towards us. Brian remained seated on the steps.

I clenched my fist, ready to slam it straight into The Bullfrog's jaw as soon as he was close enough. But as he came within speaking distance, he raised his right hand. "Look, I'm sorry about last night, I'd had a few too many to drink. Can we shake on it?"

Brian stood and extended his hand, but I butted in. "No, we can't," I said. The Bullfrog stopped dead in his tracks. I looked deep into his eyes and told him how much of a cunt he had been and how we were in this place trying to get better and that all he was doing was trying to intimidate us.

I told him he should be more careful as the residents of Gloucester House were some of the most downtrodden and lost souls he would ever meet. We had seen the worst of the world. I then pointed at Bradford John and told The Bullfrog how lucky he was that he hadn't started on John, as the last time someone had pushed him he went to prison for doing extremely bad things. A look of fear and realisation hit The Bullfrog's face and John's too, for that matter.

I sat The Bullfrog down and told him how we were at Gloucester House to get better and not to make enemies. I told him about the groups we attended, how all of us had been through the grinder and that drink had been our only way of escape. I told him how, for many of us, Gloucester House was our saving grace. I finished by telling him that instead of intimidating us he should think about being a bit kinder.

By the time I was finished The Bullfrog was fully deflated and close to tears. He explained how his father, who was a drinker, had brought him up and that he didn't like being the tough guy around the village, but that it was all he knew.

After talking to The Bullfrog for about an hour, I shook his hand and he went off to meet his friends. When he had gone, Bradford John stood up and said, "It's a good job you spoke to him, Peter, because I was just about to sort him out."

Brian and I looked at each other and burst out laughing. "Come on, Rocky," I said, "let's go and get a cuppa!"

Many people passed through Gloucester House, but few stayed the minimum recommended thirteen weeks. Those who did usually stayed a lot longer. The reality of sobriety is that nobody really gives a shit about you and your problems.

Most people are too busy dealing or not dealing with problems of their own. The biggest wake-up call you experience is how fragile your life is and how lucky you are to have survived as far as the rehab centre.

The moment I personally realised the importance of my sobriety came one Sunday evening. Brian and I were sitting in the TV room when John came in and told us there had been a new admittance to the bungalow. He looked shocked as he said it was an elderly lady. A few minutes later that shock reverberated through all of us as one of the staff told us that there was indeed a new lady, but that she wasn't old, she was only in her twenties.

Later that afternoon I briefly met the girl in the kitchen. Her body belied her age. Ravaged by drugs and drink, she had lost most of her teeth and her skin had the texture of a seventy-year-old's. And yet underneath this frail, tired-looking lady you could see remnants of a once-beautiful young woman. For one reason or another she had strayed down the path of destitution and sorrow. She spoke sweetly, but the pain in her heart showed through.

After meeting her I went back to the TV room and sat watching the television with Christian. Christian, a 'serial rehabber', had seen the inside of a rehabilitation centre more times than his therapist. His normal pattern would be to arrive after the festival season, stay through the winter months and genuinely try to get sober. But by the time the spring solstice arrived and the outdoor parties began he would be off again. Christian told me that at the last count he had been in thirty-seven rehab centres!

This was a guy who could quote *The Big Book* verbatim and read it backwards from memory. But sadly, he missed the point. He forgot that not only do you have to know it; you also have to live it. He never knew how lucky he was to get so many chances when many others get so few.

I had only just settled down when a commotion in the corridor outside the room disturbed us. An ambulance driver and a paramedic arrived and rushed into the house. Christian and I went to see what was happening, but the staff stopped us and told us to go back to the TV room. We asked what was wrong and they said that the new lady was very ill.

After a couple of minutes Brian came in, his pale face showing shock and disbelief. "She's dead," he announced.

I couldn't believe my ears. She had only been with us a couple of hours and now she was dead. She had suffered a seizure and collapsed in the bungalow. No one spoke as we rolled and lit our cigarettes. It was then, in that smoke-filled room, that I made a promise to myself. While I was here I was going to get as much information as possible. I wasn't going to leave Gloucester House only to return later as a drunk. I only wanted to be there the once.

As we sat there in shock, the girl's lifeless body was wheeled past us and into the waiting ambulance. One of the staff came in and confirmed that the young lady had died. That night a lot of people contemplated their futures and I went to bed and prayed to God that I would make it through my twelve-step programme and not end up like Christian or, worse still, like the young girl; another statistic of fatal failure.

Nineteen

Life on the Outside

The daily group sessions became more and more difficult and tears often flowed, but people were getting better. My attitude had changed and it was no longer all doom, gloom and lemonade. I had begun to see a positive future. Brian, John and I started to go to church again on a Sunday and made a few friends among the locals.

It was the height of summer and most nights after group therapy we played golf at the local course or went to the outdoor swimming pool. My new eating habits meant I had put on weight and my thinking had changed radically thanks to the twelve-step programme. The only problem I had was that I was really missing my girls. I rang and spoke to Sarah, who agreed to bring Jade and Amber to visit me.

I had been at Gloucester House for almost three months and Sarah was my only contact with the outside world. I had received a phone call from one of my brothers and my mother, but apart from that there was nothing.

The girls came to see me and we spent the day at a local picnic site enjoying the food Sarah had brought with her. Sarah was always good to me and the girls treated her like a second mum. I don't how or why she put up with me, but thankfully she did. After a great day with my girls I made my promise to them that I would never drink again and told them I would be home soon. We cuddled and Sarah took them home to their mum.

That night I sat and prayed to God to keep my children safe and to give me the strength to get through. I implored him to help me become the father my girls could be proud of instead of the part-time dad who only turned up on odd weekends if he wasn't too drunk or hungover. Or both.

My mind drifted and I remembered how when I did turn up to see the girls I would usually take them to the cinema and then to a pub for waffles and ice cream. I always made it sound like a treat for them when really it was a way for me to get a few afternoon drinks in.

As I write this, I look back and think of all the time I wasted sitting in bars with my two wonderful daughters when instead we could have been doing so many better things. At the time I never gave it a second thought, but no child deserves to be stuck in a pub or parked in a beer garden and fed fizzy pop and crisps while mum, dad or both parents drink themselves stupid at the bar. I hated it when my own parents did it, yet I did the same, and out there in the world it is happening every day.

At this point I deviate from my own experiences to make a plea to any parents who do this. Don't! It's a horrible way to live and the excuse that "kids like it in the local beer garden, it's a family day out" is utter bollocks. Trust me, they don't enjoy it; they hate every moment. Next time you're propping up a bar and getting irritated because you have to check on them every five minutes and keep them in line, you should stop and think. They are screaming for your attention.

They don't want to be stuck on some cheap plastic play equipment, or sitting on the beer-soaked grass, or eating at that ash-stained table. They want *you*. They want your time and attention. They hate the fucking pub and, deep inside, maybe you do too.

***

After the visit from my girls, things just seemed to click into place and the thought or desire to drink never entered my mind. I was totally committed to my twelve-step work and attended AA regularly. Group sessions were getting easier to handle and I opened up more than ever.

During a one-to-one session with Dave, my counsellor, we spoke about my future and I told him I wanted to go to college to get some qualifications. He thought this was a good idea and suggested I look into it further. I had no intention of going back to my home town and decided to look for a course in the local area. I learned that City of Bath College had an open day coming up so I asked David, the manager, if I could go along.

As I walked through the historic city of Bath, its majestic buildings, wide streets and overall beauty gobsmacked me. At the college I spoke to a representative regarding a music course. They were happy to enrol me for the following September, so all I needed was somewhere to live. I searched high and low, but sadly to no avail. This gutted me as I had had my heart set on living in Bath and looked forward to starting the course. But as there was nothing I could do, I spoke to Dave and decided that if I couldn't go to Bath I would have to return to Loughborough.

Dave didn't agree. He thought I would be better off away, starting afresh in a new home. But I was adamant and a week later I was back in my home town.

At first I lived in bed and breakfast accommodation, but after a few weeks the council housed me in a flat on a rundown estate. The excitement at being back soon wore off and the happiness I had felt at coming this far began to wane. I met up with a few of my old mates in the pub where we used to hang out and spent the entire night drinking lemonade. Being in the pub was stupid as it was dangerous for my sobriety, but I knew no other way of living. I was already slipping back into my old routine, just minus the alcohol. I was the proverbial dry drunk!

I now saw my friends and the people I knew in a different light. The shine that used to sparkle in the many venues I had frequented had dimmed. Instead of glowing, happy people, all I saw now were soulless figures following the same old routine of working all day and drinking all night.

I became confused and unhappy. I could feel my old depression dragging me back into its clutches once more. I wondered if I had done the right thing leaving Gloucester House when I did. I visited Sarah and thanked her for her help. She had moved on with her life and I respected that and wished her well. By getting me into rehab she had saved my life.

After a few weeks of living dry and feeling unhappy, I began to decorate my flat in the hope that this positive act would lift me, but it didn't. Halfway through I sat down and wondered if this was all that life had to offer. In Highworth I had had my moment of clarity and had such high hopes that the changes I made to my life meant that a new beginning had dawned. So why weren't things different now? That night I lay in my bed and cried myself to sleep.

The next day I should have taken delivery of a sofa I had bought, but I found out it had arrived and had subsequently gone missing. My neighbour tipped me off that the lads in the flat next door had taken it. I was furious. How dare they take my stuff?

In my temper, and without thought of the consequences, I took a claw-hammer from under the sink. I went into the block next to mine and gently tapped on the door of the lads' flat. It was only about 7.30am, so I knew they would be home. One of these lads was gay and liked to smoke pot in large quantities. I guessed they had probably been up all night smoking and playing music. I tapped again.

"Who is it?" a camp-sounding voice called out. I had to think fast if I was going to get him to open the door. "Postman," I said. "Recorded delivery and what looks like a giro."

The door opened and in front of me stood a tall, skinny, blond-haired lad who went white with fright at the sight of me. I grabbed him hard around the throat, held the hammer up high and asked him where his mate was. He pointed to the bedroom. I felt sorry for them, but I was infuriated that they had stolen my sofa.

I walked into the bedroom and peered at the lad who was asleep in bed. Something had taken over me and I wanted to smash his head in there and then, but I took hold of my feelings and stopped myself from doing something stupid. Instead, I decided to scare him. I took the hammer and started tapping 'sleeping beauty' on the forehead with it and quietly calling his name. He opened his eyes and froze with shock when he saw me towering over him with a hammer pointed at his face.

"I'm sorry. I didn't mean to take the sofa, I thought it was scrap," he blurted. Granted, I had bought it from a second-hand shop, but it wasn't scrap and it wasn't his. It was mine. I told him that he had until that evening to return the money I had spent on the sofa and that if he didn't I wouldn't be waking him up with the hammer. I would be putting him to sleep with it.

Every limb in my body shook as I returned to my flat, not with temper, but as if a shock too great to handle had come my way. I turned to my new nectar and made a pot of tea, but I recognised inside of me a familiar urge, which tried to tell me I needed a drink of much stronger proportions.

I stood stirring my tea for an age, contemplating what I had just done. I knew my actions weren't the right ones and questioned how, after all I had learned, I could take such a course. The realisation came to me that I wasn't yet ready for life on my own. I went to a telephone box and spoke to Dave at Gloucester House. I told him I was unhappy and that life wasn't working out as planned. He asked me if I had drunk alcohol again. I could honestly answer no.

"Right, head straight back here," he told me. Relief mingled with shock. After all, I had felt ready for the outside world and here I was crawling back to Gloucester House within such a short space of time. But I knew that if I didn't, the proverbial 'hitting the bottle' would be my fate once more.

Later that day one of the lads came around with half of the money for the sofa. I called my friend Justin, the son of my old boss Bill from Sammy's, and without hesitation he agreed to give me a lift back to Gloucester House.

Twenty

My Epiphany

I had a meeting with Dave and Sue on my return and they allocated me a room in a halfway house in Highworth village. From then on, I had to live under the same strict rules but look after myself, only going back to Gloucester House for group sessions and Sunday lunch.

Although I had only been away from Gloucester House for a few weeks I found that most of the residents I knew had moved on. Brian was still around and another previous resident called Gordon, but they now lived in flats and only visited Gloucester House for group work.

On moving into the halfway house I set up my small room. I placed pictures of my daughters on the windowsill and my small radio on the bedside cabinet. I looked around with mixed emotions. The cosy feel of the place reminded me of the room I had had in Manor Drive when I was about fifteen. That night this one-time house DJ fell asleep listening to *Graham Torrington's Late Night Love*.

The group session the next day had a different feel to it. The dynamic of the group had changed, as had the atmosphere at Gloucester House. Some of the new residents seemed suspicious of me and as soon as I introduced myself the questions began to fly my way. They wanted to know why I had returned. I told them about the incident and how I had dealt with it and said that life outside Gloucester House was harder than they thought. I sensed an air of disdain.

Danny, a small-framed, tattooed skinhead who sat next to

Brian, laid into me. He asked if I thought I was a hard man. I didn't like his attitude and my first thoughts were of the hammer back at the flat. But I was back here to stay sober, so I listened to what he had to say. He instantly labelled me, telling me he had met my type before and that I wasn't as hard as I thought I was. I reeled with confusion. What the fuck did this little shit know? He had never met me before and here he was telling me and the rest of the room who he thought I was.

My old friend Brian butted in. I thought he was going to defend me, but instead he let out a scathing attack about how I had always thought that I was better than everyone else and declared that I must have been drinking to end up back there. His remarks stunned me. I couldn't believe someone I had spent so many good times with and been through so much with could turn on me. I left the room in tears and sat in the TV lounge. After a while Brian came in and apologised for his outburst. It was then that I noticed a puncture mark on his arm and knew that he was using again.

I became an outcast at Gloucester House and didn't want to mix with anyone. Instead of hanging around laughing and joking with the rest of them, I just studied *The Big Book* and attended meetings. I hated Gloucester House and everyone in it the second time around and in a one-to-one session with Dave I told him so. In his infinite wisdom he told me he was glad because it meant that I wouldn't want to come back for a third time.

On returning to the halfway house from an AA meeting one evening I heard noises coming from my housemate's room. Those running the facility frowned on us starting new relationships while in recovery and one of their rules stated that there must be no sex between residents. The reason for this is that one of the biggest causes of relapse for AA members is getting involved in intimate relationships too soon. There is a saying in AA that "the odds of finding a relationship in AA are good, but the goods are odd".

After years of rejection, people in recovery can fall in love too easily and any small amount of affection may feel like true love. This can cause a confusion of emotions for a person who has spent years and often decades feeling unwanted.

It was common knowledge that my housemate and one of the female residents were close, but the noise coming from the room next door confirmed that they were having a full-on relationship. This realisation made me angry because, despite being very different people, we were getting on well. Knowing how bad this relationship was for them both and how it could cause either or both of them to relapse, I felt they had put me in a bad position. Later that afternoon, and to the disgust of the rest of the group, I challenged them about what I had heard. The manager summoned them to the office.

I had meant no malice in bringing their relationship to the attention of the group; I had only sought to save their recovery. Everyone else saw it in a different light and over the course of the next few weeks they totally ostracised me.

It didn't really matter as my mind had changed and I knew I had progressed in my thinking, whereas these people looked at me through the eyes of addicts. I understood and knew how it felt for them as I had been there myself.

After a couple more months of group therapy I began to tolerate the other residents, but I spent less and less time with them. I didn't enjoy their company and the feeling was mutual. I now attended more AA meetings outside Gloucester House than I did in it and I knew that profound changes had taken place inside of me.

One autumn evening the lad I shared the house with invited some other residents from Gloucester House round, so I decided to go out. I was feeling low and knew a walk would be the best thing for me. I headed towards the golf course.

The setting of the sun clothed the greens and the trees in an orange glow. I basked in the remnants of its warmth as I sat on one of the practice greens. The sound of the woodland animals going about their business in the small wood behind me added to the peaceful feel of this perfect evening. I rolled myself a cigarette, enjoying the fresh tobacco smell. As I blew a thin line of smoke out and my body relaxed I looked into the distance, where the last of the sun had sent beams of light onto the putting green, bathing it in a beautiful golden hue. I saw a man tap his ball into the hole and the dream of my father revisited me.

I sat up and, like a scene from a Disney movie, hundreds of baby rabbits emerged from the wood with their mothers. The young rabbits hopped and played while their mothers sat and groomed.

A peace like I have never known entered me and I knew this was my personal epiphany. I could feel the presence of my dad and I wept. Tears of joy ran down my face. A happiness I had never felt before came to me and I knew without doubt that a new life was possible and that my old life was now firmly in the past. Cleansed and with my spirit reawakened I was ready to take this chance to start again.

The next day I sat in the office with Dave and Sue. They asked me how I felt. I told them that I couldn't live with the people in that house any longer. I thought they were all mad. I told him they were a bunch of lost souls living a lie. Dave smiled and looked at Sue, who also smiled.

I asked Dave what they were grinning about. He said: "You're right. They are, but you are not; not anymore." With that, he and Sue told me I was ready to go home.

A week later my friend Justin came and picked me up to take me home. I moved into a new flat on Tuckers Road in Loughborough and yet again started over. I decorated my new home and in the evenings I walked around a local nature reserve and took in the fresh air.

On weeknights I attended AA. I read my AA books on a daily basis and kept in touch with other recovering alcoholics to aid my recovery. This time I was determined not only to stay sober, but to live my life differently. At night I said my childhood prayers and in the mornings I read my books. I distinctly remember sitting in bed one night sipping hot chocolate and reading my AA book. I giggled out loud when I realised it was 10.30pm on a Saturday night and here I was tucked up in bed!

I was happy in my new flat and life was going well. I was back in contact with my children, eating healthily and sticking to my AA routine. But inside something was missing.

Working at the nightclub with my brother John.

A few years before rehab: The drink had taken control

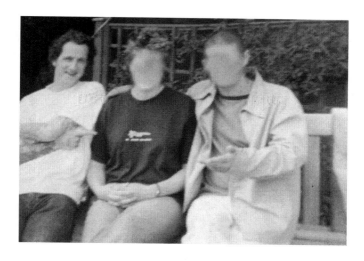

Me, Brian and Julie Andrews: relaxing in the rehab garden.

Me and Brian waiting for the bullfrog.

Peter Skillen

Twenty One

The Angel of Death

Once again I looked in the wrong place for the missing link; for that something to help me lift the deep depression that enveloped my waking hours. By doing so I broke the rule I had tried to save a fellow inmate from. I got into a relationship.

And just as the advice says, I found my new found emotions of being a recently dry addict ran too deep. I jumped into the relationship for all the wrong reasons. I wanted to feel loved. After all, didn't I deserve that now that I had changed my ways?

I mistook my feelings for love, whereas the girl I was with saw it as a bit of fun. On reflection, I was a bit of a fool to think it was anything more, but I was new to the world and wanting love.

The relationship ended and I felt foolish to have let myself be drawn into something I had been warned about so many times in rehab. I rang Dave. After listening to what had happened and how it had all affected me, his advice was to buy a plant. *A plant?* I was more dumbfounded than ever.

"Yeah, a bloody plant. And when you've learnt to water and feed that and you've watched it grow, you might be ready for a pet, but you aren't ready for a relationship. Stick to the plant, women are far too complicated a thing for you to be dealing with yet, my boy."

I laughed. It was good to hear Dave's unique way with words once more. I should have discussed other feelings with him, as that night I was in need of company and like the idiot I seemed to be at that time I went to the last place I should have: the pub. However, it did open my eyes to the way some people felt about me and how unforgiving they can be.

It was around half-past eight on a Sunday evening when I walked into the pub. I had heard that the local bar held an acoustic night on Sundays and that a few old friends frequented it, so I thought it would be a good idea to go and join them to try and lift my spirits. A night of lemonade and good company was all I needed.

The place was buzzing. I ordered my lemonade at the packed bar and stood in the corner looking around to see if I could see any of my friends. Instead of the euphoria that I thought would visit me, an uncomfortable feeling settled. The bright lights and fun – which in the past had filled me with anticipation and excitement – paled, until all I noticed was the acrid smell of sweat and smoke and how ridiculously drunk everyone was. *Is this really what life was all about?*

I made my way towards the toilet and on the way bumped into an old friend who had a couple of girls with him. He asked me to join them as the two birds were up for it. Fed up of sitting in the corner, I agreed. I remembered the two girls from around town and they instantly recognised me.

When I came back and joined them my friend pushed a cocktail towards me. "Here you go, mate, get that down your neck," he said.

I would be lying to say that I wasn't tempted, but I resisted my old urges and explained to him that I was off the beer. One of the girls interrupted: "Yeah right, pull the other one."

I smiled, ignoring the obvious distain in her voice. I then explained about my recent trip to rehab. My friend offered his apologies and told me he had no idea. The very drunk girl scoffed at my story. "I don't believe a word of it," she said. "You, Pete Skillen, changed and stopped drinking? That's a joke, innit?"

I had never had anything to do with the girl before, so her attitude made me feel confused and angry. Why would she have any reason to disbelieve me? It came to me then that my decision to go to the pub was the wrong one and that the company I was in was unforgiving. I had to get out of there, so I said my goodbyes and left.

My depression came back with a vengeance. I made my way to the local kebab shop, but as I stood waiting for my food I had a moment of clarity. My problem was that I was living the life of a dry drunk. Again I had slipped into old habits, minus the beer. I left the kebab shop without my food and walked towards my home.

The town centre had a quiet, eerie feel that only a Sunday night can give it. Giggles coming from behind me broke the silence. I ignored them, not thinking they were for my benefit, until without warning they turned to scorn and abuse. Looking round I saw the two girls I had met in the pub. I said hello, but they rebuffed my friendly greeting and returned with a vitriol of hate. "Who the fuck do you think you are?" one shouted.

To say that I was taken aback by this silver-tongued female, and I use the word *female* in the loosest possible way, was an understatement. In fact, her outburst stopped me dead in my tracks. I asked her what her problem was with me. She said that she had heard all about the Skillens and all about me. To her and her ilk, she stated, "the Skillens are the scum of Loughborough".

Her words triggered a wave of anger in me, but she hadn't finished, and this time her frail-looking, sweet-faced friend joined her: "You lot are a bunch of fucking gypsies. You think you're fucking tough, but you're not. Go on, hit me then."

Shell-shocked by their hate-filled comments, I just stood looking at them as the scorn continued. And then one of them drew back and spat straight into my face. My humiliation and rage urged me to smack her clean in the mouth, but I held my temper, turned my back and walked.

As I did so, I wiped away not only her spittle that had run down my cheek, but also the tears that were streaming from my eyes. I cried all the way home. When I arrived I washed my face, lifted my head and looked in the mirror. Disbelief and sadness looked back at me. The vile encounter had brought me to one of my lowest points since leaving the safety of the rehab centre. I wondered if it was worth it.

The next morning I awoke and made my way to the martial arts and fitness centre my brother John had opened. John knew I was finding it hard to cope and introduced me to one of his friends, Colin. John confided in Colin about how I had been struggling with life on the outside and Colin kindly offered to have a word with me as he had come through massive adversity in his own life.

We left the gym and went to a local café for a cuppa and a chat. Colin told me about the problems he had been through in his life. Believe me when I say that many a man would have crumbled under the pressure of his experiences. But Colin had forged a strong character and a will of iron through many a battle.

After he had finished his tale he sat upright and moved close to me. His face changed and his eyes pierced mine. "I'm the angel of death," he said.

A shiver ran through me and I feared what would happen next. Colin continued, "And I'm here to tell you that you've only got another twenty-four hours to live."

To be honest, I shat myself at that. Colin spoke again, "But before I take you from this life I am going to give you anything you want... anything. But let me remind you of one thing. No matter where you want to go or what you want to do, in twenty-four hours you're dead!"

My chilled spine felt like someone had brushed it with a feather. I couldn't speak. Colin looked at his watch and then tapped the dial, indicating that my time was ticking away. I started to think that Colin might actually be telling the truth.

"So," said Colin, "what do you want to do? You can do anything you wish, but you've only got twenty-three hours and fifty-nine minutes left, so you'd better hurry up."

In a panic I started to think about all the important things in my life and what I would actually miss if this were true. Colin interrupted my thoughts, tapping his watch once more. "Twenty-three hours and forty minutes..."

I began to talk. I told Colin I wanted to go and see my mum and to be with my children. Collin interjected: "Now I want you to imagine you only have twelve hours left."

"I'd want my family to surround me," was my answer.

"Six hours," came the reply.

"I'd want to make sure that my children knew how much I loved them. I'd want to say thank you to Dave and the rest of my friends from rehab."

"One hour." This time his voice urged me on.

"Er... with my kids..."

"One minute, what are you going to say?"

"I want to tell them that I love them. I want to say that I'm sorry."

"Ten seconds, nine, eight, seven, six..."

Near panic gripped me.

"Five, four, three, two..."

"But I don't want to die yet!"

Colin stopped counting. "You're one second from death, but I've changed my mind. I'm going to let you live." As he said this an excitement filled me.

Colin looked at me and said: "You can do all those things now. You can go out and do exactly what you said you wanted to do. But remember you might be just one second from death, so don't wait, do it now."

It dawned on me what he had done. Colin had made me realise that we don't know how long we have left. We may be only a second or twenty-four hours away from death at any time. Nobody knows, so why shouldn't we live our lives to the fullest? Why shouldn't we go out and do the things we really want to do?

I sat there and thanked Colin for the chat. He had singlehandedly reignited the fire in my belly. I vowed from that moment on that I was going to do the things I wanted to do. I had always been a dreamer. I had filled my long days walking along the riverside while skiving off school with dreams of becoming a Hollywood film producer. If I wasn't walking down by the river when I was skipping school, I'd be at the cinema. That was my dream. But first I had to get myself physically fit again.

Twenty Two

Turning a Negative into a Positive

In between my bouts of drinking I had kept my hand in, and my feet too for that matter, with my kickboxing training. It was nothing much to shout about, but nevertheless I still trained. As my mental stability was improving at this point, I decided I needed to get myself back into physical shape.

I paid John my three-month membership upfront and attended the gym every day. I started a daily cardio routine: first I did five minutes on the runner, then five minutes of skipping, then five minutes on the cross-trainer, then five minutes on the punch bag and finally two thousand metres on the rower. I did this daily and then eventually twice a day, gradually building up my levels over the following few weeks. It wasn't long before I had increased to ten minutes at each station and had added a heavy punch bag and some pad work into the routine.

After about a month I had built up to fifteen minutes per station and was finishing each two-hour session with thirty minutes on the bag with the addition of a weight training set on alternate days. As I said before, I have never been the biggest of lads, but these routines made me strong and more importantly they forged my mind.

I developed a steely determination and began to set myself goals. I had almost reached the point of taking my black belt on a couple of occasions in the past but had always given up. Psychologically, I had never thought myself worthy of wearing the treasured black belt, so I grabbed the first excuse I could to avoid it. But this time I had the determination to prove my worth and to one day have a black belt of my own.

I had trained hard previously, but at this time I pushed myself through mental as well as physical barriers. This proved more important for me than any other training I had done. Kickboxing once again featured in my life and a fire lit up within me during sparring sessions. I felt good. I was fit, strong and had a real passion for my training. Now I was hill-sprinting, kickboxing and hitting the bag and pads; my cardio had gone through the roof. I knew the time had come, as physically and mentally I was prepared to become a black belt.

John asked me if I wanted to work a few shifts in the gym. He couldn't pay much, but he threw free training into the deal so I accepted. I opened up the gym at six each morning, did my training routine and then worked all day. In the evening I would train again. I virtually lived at my brother's gym. I attended seminars held there, studied martial arts DVDs and read countless books that influenced both my training and my new lifestyle.

One morning John told me to get ready for the next day as he wanted me to do forty rounds on the heavy punch bag. I knew that if I let the prospect of this run around in my head for a full twenty-four hours, the chances were that the thought of the challenge could become too scary and I would walk away from it as I had done when faced with such tests on many previous occasions. That thought killed me as I knew that if I failed in this, or in any trial I put myself through, I could also fail in my battle against alcoholism.

Alcoholism is such a sly disease and you have to stay on top of it at all times. It is the only illness that tells you that you haven't got it. Show it the slightest chink in your AA armour and it will start to crawl back into your life, slowly but surely.

With this thought strong in my mind, I told myself: *Fuck it, I'll do the rounds right now.* I turned to my brother. "No time like the present," I said. And then, with a smile imprinted on my face at how decisive I sounded, I changed and got stuck straight into the heavy bag. More than two hours later I had completed forty-one three-minute rounds. Despite my hands swelling and radiating with pain, I felt good and knew that the previous weeks of dedicated training had held me in good stead.

A week later, John hit me with another challenge. We drove to Huddersfield to train world-renowned martial artist Peter Consterdine (8th dan; the highest attainable rank). This was a Thursday morning session and we worked alongside some of the hardest hitters and best fighters in the world of martial arts.

I couldn't help making comparisons. Up until this point I had lived a fairly meaningless life and lost everything that was dear to me, but by this point I was on a different path. I no longer woke up in my own puke, sifted through empty beer bottles or scraped for cigarette butts. Now I jumped out of bed at six every morning and made my way to the 'dojo'; the matted area I trained in.

I had broken my chains and trained long and hard. Plus, being with John, Peter and the rest of the magnificent martial artists, I knew that I was walking with giants. I had reached the pinnacle of my journey to that point and stood proud, surrounded by some of the best martial artists the martial arts world has to offer.

Watching these warriors as they prepared themselves for the session ahead, time seemed to slow down, my heartbeat drummed in my ears and I could hear the sound of my own breathing. I smiled and asked myself,

"How the fuck did I get here?"

I loved training with Peter. For more than two hours I sweated, punched and kicked with the best of them and held my own. I was in my element for every second of it and it made me feel so alive. That session inspired me to seek out other instructors and clubs to train with. I travelled to seminars and trained with some of the best instructors in the world.

At last I was due to take my black belt. There was no room for any more avoidance. This was my ultimate challenge and I was ready for it. As well as doing all my set punching, kicking and cardio routines, I was to fight three rounds of boxing with Amateur Boxing Association (ABA) Area Champion Wayne Finney and ten rounds of kickboxing with some of the black belts from my brother's club.

The kicking and punching went well, but the eight rounds on the bag were exhausting. I pushed my body harder than ever before and felt the strain in every fibre of my being, but my mind stayed strong and I wouldn't allow myself to give up.

As I faced up to Wayne, all the old feelings of fear came flooding back. Wayne is a first-class heavyweight with hands like lightening and a punch that would upset the Richter scale. But it wasn't him I feared. I feared failure. I was frightened of coming this far and then falling at the final hurdle. I took a deep breath and started sparring.

Wayne toyed with me at first, letting the odd flurry of punches go every now and then. This lad is a boxer of repute, a master with his hands. He jabbed, hooked and crossed my head and body more times that I cared to count. I threw a high volume of punches and lasted the three rounds, but outweighed and outclassed I received the best boxing lesson of my life.

After these rounds, my great friend Wayne Harper took me to one side. Wayne and his brother Lee are without doubt the finest friends anybody could wish for. Years ago when times were hard and food in our house was short, Lee and his friend Mario, who worked at a local fish and chip shop, always saw us right for food. The Harper brothers are the type of friends who you may not see for years, but when you do it's like you saw them the day before. They are both true gentlemen, with hearts of gold and fists of iron.

Wayne had thought for years that I deserved my black belt and had always made a point of telling me so. When he found out that I was finally taking it, he came to support me. I was tired, but I still had ten rounds of kickboxing to go. Wayne padded me up and gave a speech to fire me up. He told me not to forget how far I had come and to never give up.

I stood and started my semi-contact rounds of kickboxing. Semi-contact soon turned into almost full contact and the fights got tougher. I dug deep, but in the third round I hit out with a punch and caught the head of my opponent. I heard a loud crack and knew instantly that my hand was broken. My brother asked me if I wanted to stop, but I wouldn't. I had come this far and wasn't going anywhere.

Wayne again took me to one side and reminded me of how I had got to where I was. I sucked in a deep breath and, with a broken hand, an aching body and burning lungs, I picked up the gauntlet and started to fight again. I fought out the remainder of the rounds using only my feet. I pulled off a range of spinning kicks, axe kicks, back kicks, jumping kicks and finished the final round with a scissor takedown. I had accomplished everything that had been asked of me and achieved one of the goals that had eluded me for so long.

As I stood in the centre of the room the following week receiving my beautiful, gold-embroidered black belt, the years of heartache, loneliness and pain simply melted away into insignificance. I knew this wasn't the end of a journey; it was the start of a whole new beginning.

over the years since being in recovery I have trained with some of the best martial artists alive and achieved multiple dan grades from them. Just as importantly, I have taken myself back to the bottom of the ladder to learn new disciplines.

These new disciplines are teaching me more and more about myself and reinforcing the belief in me that every time we put ourselves into the forge we come out stronger and sharper. Our steely resolve is enhanced through training in these arts. Martial arts can give you what you need to continue with your journey, no matter how hard it may be. These disciplines toughen our minds and our bodies.

Epilogue

I have sat in rooms across the length and breadth of the country listening to people just like me; people who have shared their deepest and darkest fears; people who were once trapped in the dark but are now bathed in light and living amazing lives.

Some of these people have travelled the world. Some have become artists, sculptors or poets. Some are still on the path to a better life. And some did not make it and are sadly no longer with us. But I know that everyone who *tries* is on the right path. I know this because I am still walking this path. My journey is no longer about waste and decay; it is about walking towards the light.

Every time I wrap that black belt around my waist the dark days of my life come to the front of my mind. Every time I look into those nine stitched rows of silky blackness, it reminds me of a past full of darkness. But the gold stitching emblazoned on the blackness reminds me that I did it! If *I* can do it, *you* can do it. With faith, commitment, dedication and hard work, mixed with some blood, sweat and tears, *anyone* can find light in the darkness and learn to live again.

As you have read, my life to date has been somewhat colourful. Over the years, I have seen and been involved in violence on a grand scale. I have lost time I can never get back and sometimes nightmares from my past still terrify me.

But I have learned how to deal with circumstances beyond my control and to survive circumstances that would grind many people to dust. I hang on in there because deep down inside I know that my life has purpose. I always knew that one day I would be able to serve others, and if that service helps to release just one person from the chains that bound me in the past then my life has been worth living.

There were many points in my life when I wanted to give up. As a child, I was so depressed that I thought the future could hold nothing but pain. Sometimes it did, but along the way I had my fun. I have walked along sun-drenched beaches, danced until the small hours, laughed with true friends and had experiences that some people can only ever dream about. But when the bad times outweigh the good there is no choice but to stop and take stock. It was time for me to take a long look at my life and ask one simple question: was it all worth it?

Well, the answer for me is simple. No, it wasn't. Every last second I spent turning my back on those who cared about me and drinking myself into oblivion was a complete waste of time. I missed watching my two eldest daughters grow up and I lost so many things that I can never get back.

All I can say to you is this: do yourself a huge favour and don't make the same mistakes I did. The simple promise I made to myself when I got sober was that I would try my best, my very best, to be a better man.

That means achieving goals and passing on a message of hope to others. There is always time to turn your life around, achieve your dreams, find love, be there for those who need you and be happy. So get up, get out there, become somebody, do great things and achieve your dreams.

But do it *now!*

Peter Skillen, *The Twelve-Step Warrior*

Peter still lives in Loughborough and is in his twelfth year of sobriety. He continues to uphold the AA's twelve-step programme of recovery that changed his life.

Peter now holds a BSc honours degree and works with young adults, helping them achieve their dreams. He has achieved multiple black belts from some of the most respected martial arts practitioners teaching today and continues to pass this knowledge on through his own classes. He has designed bespoke training regimes for the general public, corporate clients, educational establishments, and world and Olympic sports champions.

Peter welcomes feedback and communication with readers of *The Twelve-Step Warrior*. You can contact him at

Facebook group: Peter Skillen Author

Twitter: @12stepwarrior

Post Word

Written by addiction counsellor David Reed

ADDICTION

"Addictus - a citizen of Ancient Rome who had built up debts that could not be repaid and was therefore delivered by the courts into slavery under his creditor. That heroin and cocaine are potential slave masters few would question but are alcohol and tobacco to be feared in the same way? And what about tea, or sugar, or gambling?"

(Robson, 1999)

"Hell is our natural home. We have lost everything. We live in fear of living.

"Alcohol was my only friend. We found ourselves in alcohol and then it turned against us and tried to kill us. No other friend would do that to you but we kept drinking because we had to."

(Denzin, 1987)

"That humanity at large will ever be able to dispense with Artificial Paradises seems very unlikely."

(Aldous Huxley)

"I was teetotal until Prohibition"

(Groucho Marx)

I was thrilled when Peter asked me to contribute to his book. "Write something academic about addiction, Dave," he said. He then added, "About 2000 words."

This was a mixed blessing. It gave me something to aim for, but it immediately caused a sense of panic in me because a reasonably researched piece of work would run into volumes.

I immediately wondered what comes into peoples' minds when they see the word 'addiction'. In most cases, the association is with drugs such as heroin or cocaine, which can be traced back over a considerable period.

Kandall (1996) and Wanigaratne, Wallace et al (2006) regard the following as addictive behaviours: problem drinking, gambling, addictive sexual behaviours, overeating, criminal reoffending, drug use, smoking and compulsive spending. They add: "This is by no means an exhaustive list."

So, how to start? My own background is working within the (so-called) abstinence model pioneered by Alcoholics Anonymous.

This model (programme) takes the view that if a particular substance (alcohol) or behaviour seriously blights the life of the 'user' and those around him, then common sense – if nothing else – would suggest that it is best to leave the stuff alone, period.

Of course, in the case of alcohol, the social and peer pressures are enormous and my local supermarket occupies far more shelf space with alcohol than with any other category of product. My wife complained recently that several cases of cut-priced strong lager were (no doubt) strategically placed in front of the freshly roasting chicken area.

She accosted someone in a suit who, to be fair, remarked, "It isn't helpful is it?" and promised to bring this to the attention of the manager of that section. So far so good, except that nothing has changed. "We often have special deals with particular suppliers and they want the best possible chance of selling..."

The tobacco counter is no more, and tobacco is sold at the checkout with its various health warnings. So far, there is no obvious (at least!) display of cannabis, speed or 'Charlie' (cocaine)... That's a different thing altogether, I suppose!

I am 'writing' this using my laptop. I don't (as yet) feel any cravings or obsessional thoughts that 'make' me log onto porn sites, betting sites or to spend money I haven't got. However, instances of these behaviours as 'addictions' are being acted out regularly in society.

Equally, I don't anticipate finding myself, several hours from now, surfing the net or poring over so-called social networking sites, but for many that *has* become an 'addictive' behaviour, having a massive negative impact on their lives and on the lives of those around them. Indeed, on a recent news programme I heard someone mention 'Facebook addiction'.

When I started in the 'industry' of treating people who are suffering with addictions, it was far more clear-cut. If someone was clearly an 'addict' or an 'alcoholic', abstinence was the advice and the thrust of counselling.

Today, the very terms 'alcoholic' and 'addict' are considered by those who know about these things to be discriminatory and 'non-PC'. I couldn't possibly comment. Meanwhile, the media talks about 'workaholics', 'sexaholics' and so on. Serious practitioners now regard eating disorders as 'addictive behaviours', so I suppose that is something.

Within the field, other descriptions are applied to different behaviours and to different people. Thus we encounter the 'abuse' of drugs, substance 'misuse' and perhaps the most confusing of all, drug or substance 'dependency', which is not necessarily considered the same as addiction.

Where is alcohol in all of this? It is most certainly a drug, and perhaps the fellowship of AA will one day be known as 'Alcohol Addicts'.

Well, what *is* addiction, then? We will need more than two thousand words to offer a view and considerably more than that to accommodate those who will not agree. Perhaps we could start by looking at what it is *not*. It is not necessarily addiction when someone drinks 'too much' on a daily basis. It depends on how compulsive that behaviour is and the effect it has on that individual's life.

In this vein, I noticed the following in a pamphlet produced by Cambridgeshire and Peterborough NHS Foundation Trust, which gives details of a particular prescribed antidepressant drug:

Question: Is 'X' addictive?

You may experience some 'discontinuance' effects if you suddenly stop taking 'X' after several weeks. This is the body's adjustment reaction, but it does not mean you are addicted.

People taking 'X' do not get these signs of addiction:

- A need to take larger doses to get the same effect

- Experience psychological 'craving' for 'X'

- Unable to control their drug use - it is the focus of their life

- Continues to take the drug even if it harms their health

Ramsay, Gerada et al (2005) claim that people who use drugs very frequently may develop a dependence syndrome or addiction. This is when a person experiences some or all of the following changes:

- Difficulty in controlling drug-taking behaviour

- A withdrawal state when the drug use has ceased or been reduced

- A strong desire or compulsion to take the drug

- Increased tolerance to the drug, so that larger amounts are needed to achieve the desired effect

- Progressive neglect of other pleasures or interests

- Increased time spent getting the drug or recovering from its effects

- Persistence with drug use in spite of clear evidence of harmful consequences

Beck, Wright et al (1993) argue that when a drug or alcohol is taken to relieve stress-related or naturally occurring tension, anxiety or sadness, it tends to reinforce the belief "I need the drug" as well as "I can't tolerate unpleasant feelings".

Among healthcare professionals, people who have problems with alcohol or drug use are not popular. Views such as "it's a self-inflicted condition" are common.

Weegman and Cohen (2002) claim that there is now a wealth of opinion that suggests that addiction is a **biopsychosocial disorder.** It is included as a group of diseases by the World Health Organization in *The Tenth Revision of The International Classification of Diseases and Related Health Problems.*

In *Group Psychotherapy and Addiction*, **Reading and Weegman (2004), Gillian Woodward** prefers to describe "alcohol dependence - the condition or syndrome". She comments: "Alcohol dependency appears to develop in response to a combination of influences: early object relations, psychodynamic roots, politico-socio-cultural factors and genetic disposition.

"In its acute form it might be seen as a form of regression to infantile fixation points and the acting out of distress arising from earlier, unmet needs. This distress is initially alleviated by the anaesthetizing properties of alcohol, but as the (addiction) progresses, a second level of distress is created: physiologically, mentally emotionally and spiritually. Symptoms may emerge, such as intense anxiety, extreme mood swings, or paranoia, which can easily be confused with deeper more fixed problems such as bipolar disorder."

She continues: "As a psychosocial therapist working with highly dependent, newly abstinent clients, one of the frameworks that I have found useful has been **Elliot's (1997; 2003)** description of four fundamentally psychological problematic characteristics, which closely resemble features of borderline personality disorder:

- The speed and intensity with which a new dependency is formed
- The tendency towards extremes and splitting
- The preoccupation with boundaries, limits and authority and a rather 'adolescent' feel to the relationship
- Low self-esteem and below-average tolerance of emotional discomfort

To these I would add shame and the drive to self-sabotage."

Robson (1999) proposes that being 'addicted' is to be caught up in the following sequence:

- An increasingly pressing desire to carry out some activity

- Growing anxiety

- Ever-increasing mental preoccupation if this is resisted or prevented

• A sudden and highly rewarding elimination of tension and desire as the act is carried out

• As the glow of satisfaction wears off, a resumption of the cycle all over again

There are people whose work compulsion is as devastating to family life as any heroin habit.

Dusty Miller (2005) suggests that self-harming is an addiction and should be treated as such; as should eating disorders. She goes on to discuss "addictive personality disorders", while **Nakken (1996)** develops the concept of "the addictive personality". Such conclusions are universally rubbished in academic literature.

Davison, Neale and Kring (2004) write: "We have seen that 'problem drinking' is sometimes associated with other mental disorders, in particular with anxiety disorders, mood disorders and psychopathy. Therapists of all orientations have to recognise that depression is often comorbid with alcohol abuse, and that suicide is also a risk."

Forrest (1996) argues that: "Chemically dependent people are generally impulsive, act out, manifest low frustration tolerance and behave in a manipulative, irresponsible, immature, egocentric manner."

I think of what I have seen and experienced over the last fifteen years or so during my involvement in 'the industry'. I immediately feel constrained, to be honest, and say that my professional (and other) involvement has been with people whose lives have been so catastrophically ruined by their use of whatever substance, that to describe them as having abused or misused substances or of being 'chemically dependent' is, frankly, not to see or appreciate what their behaviour has done.

I am used to dealing with people who have 'lost' (some would say 'thrown away') spouses, children and wider family; all financial and material resources; careers; homes; health (physical and mental); self-respect; any place in the community; identity; and very often even accommodation. I have been to, and continue to go to, far too many funerals.

I have often found myself in a group of 'addicts' (of whatever chemical or behavioural complexion) and I'm struck by the all-too-depressing and inevitable similarities in their stories. I have no difficulty, and neither does the literature, in tracing the progression of addiction in people from one 'stage' to another and to the distressing rock bottom situations perhaps most eloquently described in:

Alcoholics Anonymous (Chapter 11: "A Vision for You")

"He cannot picture life without alcohol. Some day he will be unable to imagine life either with alcohol or without it. Then he will know loneliness such as few do. He will be at the jumping-off place. He will wish for the end."

So, again, just what *is* addiction? Peter's own story catalogues so many of the classic components that offer a susceptibility to addiction. It is all there: fears and doubts about security, personal identity and belonging; a sense of being 'less than'; a desperate need to feel acknowledged; a need to belong and to fit in. Adopting a life that is incredibly dangerous and the inevitable abuse and cruelty suffered, and yet feeling a deep need to justify and believe that it is 'cool'. Then the long 'slide' down into a world described above, the agonising humiliation and pain and, finally, an intervention, which at least stopped the relentless wheel of addiction.

Alcohol abuse (problem drinking?) has been looked at from various perspectives over the years. Many still regard it as a moral issue, a lack of self-control, while the concept of a 'disease' of alcoholism has now been around for a good while **(Jellinek: 1960).**

Rare is the person (addict) who craves and searches for an answer to something that has become part of their own pathology but is killing them without encountering mental health problems.

In his seminal work *The Divided Self,* **R D Laing** comments that people don't *have* schizophrenia, like *having* a cold. They *are* schizophrenic.

So, in my experience, it is with addicts. Some years ago I was reading Professor Anthony Clare's accounts of a long series of interviews with troubled genius Spike Milligan called *Depression and How to Survive it: Clare and Milligan* **(1994)**. At page eighty-nine my attention became focused on the observation below.

Here, Professor Clare is actually talking about what was then called *manic depression* (now referred to as *bipolar disorder*). I felt then and I feel now that his remarks could have been written about addiction, and that this is common thinking for people whose own lives have not been affected by addiction or who have not lived alongside a practising addict:

"For most people, what gives disease legitimacy, what eliminates the possibility that it is pretence or malingering, is the demonstration of a physical abnormality, an abnormal blood test, a deviant enzyme, a discrepant X-ray, a fault neurotransmitter?

"The day that a biological abnormality is found in manic depression and consistently replicated by researcher after researcher will be the day that sufferers from the disorder take their place among the so-called 'genuine' ill. Until then there will remain a question mark in the minds of many as to quite precisely what this psychiatric disorder is."

In their book, *Problem Drinking* **(Second Edition, 1989), Nick Heather and Ian Robertson** put the case against addiction being regarded as a disease, preferring a "social learning" account of alcohol use.

Similar views are expressed in *Addiction: Questions and Answers for Counsellors and Therapists* **(Reading and Jacobs, eds)** as in **Philip Flores'** *Addiction as an Attachment Disorder* **(2003).** Flores comments:

"There is an inverse relationship between addiction and healthy interpersonal attachments ... alcohol and drugs are powerfully reinforcing and inhibiting of the more subtle persuasions in a person's life ... it is rare, if not impossible, for a practising alcoholic or addict to successfully negotiate the demands of healthy interpersonal relationships."

Robson states that: "The disease/illness concept must be discarded because there are cases where 'alcoholics' do return to normal drinking."

Rutherford (1988) states that alcoholics have to give up drinking. "They have to or they die."

Gorski and Miller (1982) state that: "Chronic relapse patients will eventually die from alcoholism."

Inevitably, I have massively exceeded my allotted two thousand words, but let's look at one more definition of addiction:

From *The Healing Journey through Addiction* **(Rich and Copans, 2000)**:

"Addictions come in all shapes and forms. Although it's become popular to think of almost any behaviour that has a compulsive quality as an addiction, for our purposes an addiction is a dependency on a substance, activity, or relationship that pulls an individual away from everything else in the world.

"It is characterised by desires that consume people's thoughts and behaviours and is acted out in habitual activities designed to get the desired thing or engage in the desired activity (addictive behaviours). Unlike simple habits or consuming interests, addictions are dependencies whose consequences can seriously impair, negatively affect, or destroy, relationships, health (physical and mental) and the capacity to function effectively.

"Most of all, an addiction is debilitating. In the end, addicts are dependent on that thing that dominates their thoughts and desires and directs their behaviours; pursuit of that thing becomes the most important activity in their lives. In the advanced stages of addiction, nothing is as important as the addiction itself. For this reason, no matter what the addiction, the object of a desire may rightly be called a narcotic: a substance, activity or relationship that soothes and numbs."

Many addicts and alcoholics do achieve recovery; that is a life in which they no longer use their drugs or behaviours of choice and change their belief/value systems and behaviours. A huge element of such recovery has to be the battle against self-obsession in all its forms.

It is often achieved by an acceptance that addiction does not 'go away' and, like any potentially fatal and chronic illness, condition or syndrome, it requires handling on a daily basis. This is precisely what Peter has done and he is an inspiration to old lags (like me) in the industry.

I remember only too well Peter's arrival at rehab and have

squirmed over some of his reminders. After all, I was that "hippy type of guy in a suit".

God bless you and keep you safe, Pete.

David Reed (Marlborough, Wiltshire; October, 2011)

THE TWELVE STEPS OF ALCOHOLICS ANONYMOUS

1. We admitted we were powerless over alcohol - that our lives had become unmanageable.

2. Came to believe that a power greater than ourselves could restore us to sanity.

3. Made a decision to turn our will and our lives over to the care of God as we understood Him.

4. Made a searching and fearless moral inventory of ourselves.

5. Admitted to God, to ourselves, and to another human being the exact nature of our wrongs.

6. Were entirely ready to have God remove all these defects of character.

7. Humbly asked Him to remove our shortcomings.

8. Made a list of all persons we had harmed, and became willing to make amends to them all.

9. Made direct amends to such people wherever possible, except when to do so would injure them or others.

10. Continued to take personal inventory and when we were wrong promptly admitted it.

11. Sought through prayer and meditation to improve our conscious contact with God, as we understood Him, praying only for knowledge of His will for us and the power to carry that out.

12. Having had a spiritual awakening as the result of these steps, we tried to carry this message to alcoholics, and to practise these principles in all our affairs.

The twelve steps are reprinted with the kind permission of the General Service Board of Alcoholics Anonymous, Great Britain.

www.alcoholics-anonymous.org.uk

The AA helpline number is 0845 7697555

Glossary

Bibliography and References

Alcoholics Anonymous: The Story of How Many Thousands of Men and Women Have Recovered from Alcoholism (also known as ***The Big Book***) (2000). Alcoholics Anonymous World Services, Inc.

Davison, Gerald C; Neale, John M and Kring, Ann M (2004) ***Abnormal Psychology.*** Wiley: USA.

Denzin, N (1987) ***The Alcoholic Self.*** Sage: London.

Elliot, B (1997) ***Is the unconscious really a dirty word? New directions in the Study of Alcohol 13***: pp32-39.

Elliot, B (2003) ***Containing the Uncontainable.*** Whurr: London.

Flores, P J (2003) ***Addiction as an Attachment Disorder.*** Aronson: New York.

Forrest, Gary G (1996) ***Chemical Dependency and Antisocial Personality Disorder.*** Haworth Press: USA.

Gorski and Miller (1982) ***Counselling for Relapse Prevention.*** Independence Press: USA.

Harris, Phil (2005) ***Drug Induced: Addiction and Treatment in Perspective.*** Russell House: UK.

Heather, N and Robinson, I (1985) ***Problem Drinking.*** Oxford University Press: Oxford.

Kandall, Stephen R (1996) *Substance and Shadow: Women and Addiction in the United States.* Harvard University Press: USA.

Laing, RD (1960) *The Divided Self.* Penguin: UK.

Miller, Dusty (2005) *Women Who Hurt Themselves.* Basic Books: USA.

Milligan, S and Clare, A (1994) *Depression and how to Survive it.* Arrow: London.

Nakken, Craig (1996) *The Addictive Personality.* **Hazelden:** USA.

Ramsay, Rosalind; Gerada, Claire; Mars, Sarah; and Szmuckler, George (2005) *Mental Illness: A Handbook for Carers.* Jessica Kingsley Publishers: London.

Reading, Bill and Jacobs, Michael (eds) (2003) **Addiction: Questions & Answers for Counsellors & Therapists.** Whurr: London.

Reading, Bill and Weegman, Martin (eds) (2004) *Group Psychotherapy and Addiction.* Whurr: London.

Rich, P and Copans, Stuart (2000) *The Healing Journey Through Addiction.* John Wiley and sons: Canada.

Robson, P (1999) *Forbidden Drugs.* Oxford University Press: Oxford.

Rutherford (1988) *A Lot of Bottle.* The Institute of Alcohol Studies: London.

The ICD-10 Classification of Mental and Behavioural Disorders. World Health Organisation: Geneva.

Twerski, Abraham, J (1997) *Addictive Thinking: Understanding Self-Deception.* Hazelden: USA.

Velleman, Richard (2001) *Counselling for Alcohol Problems.* Sage: London.

Wanigaratne, Shamil; Wallace, Wendy; Pullin, Jane; Keaney, Francis; and Farmer, Roger (2006) *Relapse Behaviours for Addictive Behaviours.* Blackwell Publishing: UK.

Weegman, Martin and Cohen, Robert (eds) (2002) *The Psychodynamics of Addiction.* Wiley-Blackwell: USA.

Shelthorpe Boy.

'Never let anyone tell you you can't. You can and you should'

Peter Skillen BSc

Printed in Poland
by Amazon Fulfillment
Poland Sp. z o.o., Wrocław

53607792R00116